LOCAL WALKS
NORTH AND MID-BEDFORDSHIRE

Vaughan Basham

A comprehensive book of circular walks in this lovely rural area – a companion to the same author's collection of walks in South Bedfordshire and the North Chilterns.

Walking in the countryside is always enjoyable, but, with this book as his companion, the rambler will also be led to many interesting discoveries. An appropriate theme has been selected for every walk, and a stimulating introductory article sets the scene.

Full practical route information and comments are also provided, plus specially drawn maps.

An appendix of further walking areas includes the author's suggestions for two new long-distance circular walks.

The author, Vaughan Basham, has lived in and explored the area all his life. His keen interest in social history has led to a continuing involvement in heritage affairs, conservation projects, local organisations and charities. Scouting and the Outward Bound schools were influential in his love of the countryside and, together with his wife Una, he has always been an enthusiastic rambler.

The Book Castle

For
Una, Julian and Lorna

Second Edition Preface

When the first edition of this book appeared in 1990, the Rights of Way had only recently been revised and added to the O.S. map for North Bedfordshire. In consequence anomalies were revealed, resulting in some of the walks being modified for this new edition. Because of the Brogborough Landfill work, Walk 23 has been shortened, though I am sure the area will open up again when the Marston Vale Community Forest becomes established.

All the bus routes are updated but it is still advisable to enquire at the Bedford Bus Station for the latest information.

From feedback received, it is clear the first edition has helped people 'discover' North Bedfordshire. Its beautiful scenery contrasts markedly with the better known landscape at the southern end of the county.

First published August 1990
Revised edition published May 1994
by The Book Castle
12 Church Street, Dunstable, Bedfordshire

© Vaughan Basham

Printed in Great Britain by Antony Rowe Ltd., Chippenham

ISBN 1 871199 12 3

Cover photograph: Harrold Odell Country Park.

© **Vaughan Basham**

Contents

Contents

Introduction

After much preparatory work, both in studying maps and in checking the viability of promising routes, I have found North and Mid-Bedfordshire a more fertile walking area that at first expected, accustomed as I am to walking mainly in the Chilterns. This companion for Book I, which covered South Bedfordshire and North Chilterns, has the same format but with an emphasis on Bedfordshire as a rural county, and with agriculture as a dominant subject for discussion. Subjects you might have expected to find included here are almost certainly in Book I, the contents of which are listed in the appendices.

Many of these walks surrounding Bedford can be linked together through the guidance notes provided, so that after noting the suggested additional walking areas few 'holes' in the county should be left. All the walks can be adapted or extended, even shortened, and of course can be done in reverse or with alternative starting points chosen. Milton Bryan and Leighton Buzzard are places where both my books of walks meet.

In going out into the countryside remember to observe the Countryside Code and have a care for crops and properties, for in general farmers play their part in preserving what is after all their 'workplace'. Paths in quite a few places are kept open by ramblers on path-clearing sessions, otherwise it is the Rangers, the Wildlife Trust, the British Horse Society, the Landrover Owners Club and a few volunteers who assist farmers to look after the countryside.

N.B. Views expressed in this book are those of the author, who also takes responsibility for any errors.

Vaughan Basham

Acknowledgements

My special thanks go to John Dixon of the Bedford Ramblers who provided much county information and furnished invaluable ideas for a core of walks which acted as a 'springboard' for all the other walks devised by the author. John Lunn, Airship Industries, Beds. & Hunts. Wildlife Trust, the Bedfordshire agricultural colleges, Bedfordshire C.C., Common Ground, the Farmers' Union, Jordan's Cereals and the Rural Development Commission all provided literature – in fact, almost too much really!

Then there is Paul Bowes of the Book Castle in Dunstable who has that persuasive flair of getting Bedfordshire people to write for him on specific subjects, thus stimulating interest in Bedfordshire and the neighbouring counties.

Last, but by no means least, my wife Una who advised and encouraged me in these walks then did the proof-reading – a valuable contribution.

Vaughan Basham

British Rambling and its Origins

If British rambling has a recognisable starting date one might well offer 1740 or thereabouts and the name Robert Windham. The Grand Tour of Europe was still 'de rigueur' for every young gentleman of means as a conclusion to his education, visiting the classical sites with an intellectual travelling companion. Together with his tutor Dr. Pococke and sundry friends he engaged guides and porters in Chamonix and scaled the Swiss pine forests. They went further, venturing out onto the Mer de Glace and were probably among the first Englishmen to tread on an Alpine glacier.

Fear of mountains gave way to a spirit of eagerness. Mt. Blanc was climbed by Dr. Paccard in 1786, followed later that year by a group led by Colonel Mark Beaufoy of the Tower Hamlets Militia, and a year later another Englishman, Mr. Woodley, reached the summit. Scots and English were amongst the first conquerors of Europe's mountains, the most notable being Edward Whymper's success in climbing the 'unclimbable' Matterhorn in 1865 at his sixth attempt. The annals contain the names Smyth brothers, Forbes, Kennedy, Professor Tyndall and a host of others. Back in London the public were enthralled by Mr. Albert Smith's magic lantern shows of these alpine climbs, and Whymper's own engravings of the mountains for books of his climbing exploits provided further stimulation.

These early achievements were by enthusiasts, many of them scientists, and it was the English who organised the peasanty into an elite corps of guides and who collectively developed new climbing techniques and clothing. In a word, the English created the great sport of mountaineering which spread into all corners of the world, with the British making a speciality of the Himalayas. Little wonder that they ruled India, using Simla in the Himalayan foothills as a summer escape from the heat of the plains.

So what has all this to do with rambling? Basically it established the idea of walking for pleasure. Ladies in their long skirts over stayed foundation garments went up into the high alpine meadows (aided by tall sticks, as they could hardly bend) and out onto the fascinating glaciers. The Alpine Club in London formed in 1854 provided the aegis for these forays. Without basic rock climbing skills these summits could not have been conquered, and this sphere of activity was to become a pursuit in its own right. To get to the mountains one had to walk there, which in turn one might say laid the foundations of fell-walking.

Another influence at work was the cult of 'Romanticism'. These writers, painters and composers now embraced the countryside. Included in their number were Constable, Turner, Mendelssohn, Schubert, Sir Walter Scott and most eminent of all William Wordsworth, who more than anyone encouraged the exploration of the Lake District and Wales.

Collectively in effect they were saying, find out for yourself the joys of the countryside.

On the home scene, the Association for the Protection of Ancient Paths in the Vicinity of York came into being in 1824, followed by a crop of others all concerned with footpaths with the nationwide Commons, Open Spaces and Footpaths Preservation Society appearing in 1865 (now the Open Spaces Society), for the issues of footpaths and countryside access issues had become the bedrock of rambling (hard won as evidenced later by the great Kinder Scout Mass Trespass of 1932 in Derbyshire).

Times were when everybody walked to work either down country lanes into the farms or out of the 'back to back' industrial housing heading for the factories. Hours upon hours of toil right up into this century, so the pleasure of walking as a leisuretime pursuit for all only appears in recent times.

By the end of the nineteenth century a good number of rambling clubs were springing up, especially in the London area and the north west. Rail excursions made a contribution to this lust for walking, catering for the individual as well as the club, especially when arrangements were made between the clubs and the rail companies for concessionary fares. The companies also encouraged walking by producing special railway posters and published their own books of rambles to promote travel to distant starting-points for such walks.

Come 1931 the requirements for a national lobby looking after the needs of ramblers became evident with the Ramblers' Federation (of clubs and like-minded organisations concerned with countryside access) formed as the outcome of a meeting held in Longshaw in the Peak District. On 1st January 1935 the title changed to the Ramblers' Association, with 300 clubs and 1,200 individual members on the books. Since then the Ramblers' Association has been one of the country's leading organisations, fighting contentious issues large and small.

Between the two World Wars outdoor activities gained popular appeal, as expressed in cycling, swimming in the new municipal pools and of course walking. The Y.H.A. established a nationwide network of hostels facilitating walking holidays, and the railways provided the connections. In addition the Co-operative Holidays Association and Holiday Fellowship amongst many others offered guided walking holidays from their centres. This was also the era of the big keep-fit rallies and health camps, very much following the maxim 'healthy body – healthy mind'. Camping gained acceptance for cheap holidays as motorcycles and sidecars came into the reach of more pockets, and touring caravans took hold for those seeking fresh air away from industry.

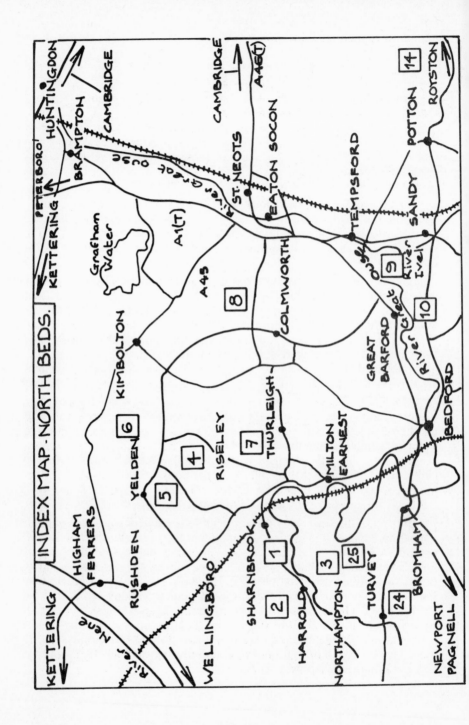

INDEX MAP - NORTH BEDS.

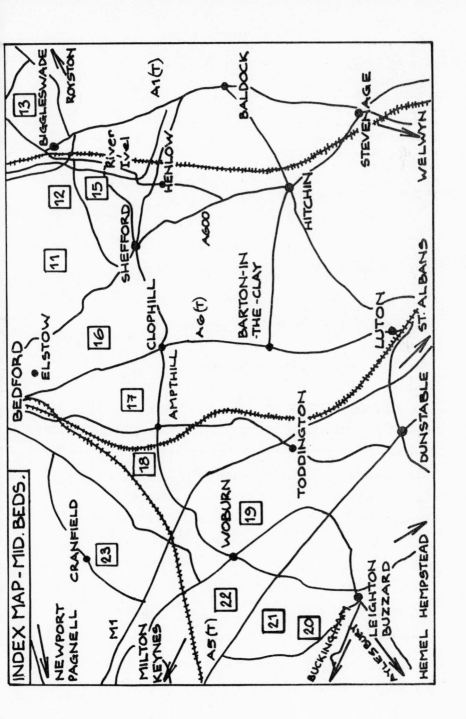

INDEX MAP - MID. BEDS.

9

The Country Code

- Guard against all risk of fire
- Fasten all gates
- Keep dogs under proper control
- Keep to the paths across farm land
- Avoid damaging fences, hedges and walls
- Leave no litter – take it home
- Safeguard water supplies
- Protect wild life, wild plants and trees
- Go carefully on country roads on the R.H.S. facing oncoming traffic
- Respect the life of the countryside

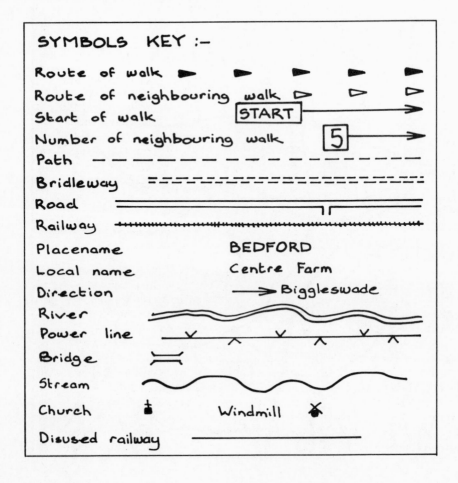

SYMBOLS KEY :–

Route of walk	► ► ► ► ►
Route of neighbouring walk	▷ ▷ ▷
Start of walk	START ──────→
Number of neighbouring walk	5 ──────→
Path	– – – – – – – – – – – –
Bridleway	= = = = = = = = = = = = =
Road	═══════════╗╔═══════
Railway	+++++++++++++++++++++++
Placename	BEDFORD
Local name	Centre Farm
Direction	──→ Biggleswade
River	
Power line	
Bridge	
Stream	
Church	♦ Windmill ✗
Disused railway	───────────

Walking in the Countryside

Places included: ODELL – FELMERSHAM – SHARNBROOK

Length of walk: 8 miles.

Grid Ref: Sheet 153 956 566.

Parking: Harrold Odell Country Park car park.

Bus services: 124, 133, 134, 135 and 136.

Public Houses: The Bell (Odell), The Mad Dog (Little Odell) and pubs in Harrold, Felmersham and Sharnbrook.

Walk Links: Walks 1, 2 and 3 all start from the Visitors' Centre, and this walk links with Walk 7 by road to the A6(T) for Bletsoe.

Notes 1: One must not fail to visit the Visitors' Centre near the Park entrance with its wealth of information particularly on birdlife with mammals and insects well represented, together with accounts of the gravel workings – the forerunner of the expanses of water. Study Groups can use the facilities and its lecture room, and the fine windows provide good views across the water. Plenty of seating around the waters for those just taking a leisurely stroll or using binoculars. Toilets are provided in the complex.
   2: See Notes for Walk 2.

WALKING IN THE COUNTRYSIDE

In making revisions for this second edition and rewalking in several areas, it is pleasing to find that paths are being left untouched and are being re-instated in quite a number of places by the farming community after they have planted their crops. Lets hope this trend accelerates and that we see the end of hedge row grubbing-out along with many more trees being planted. Bedfordshire is not too well-endowed with trees.

Bedfordshire County Council has now taken stock of its countryside with the results given in the publication 'The Bedfordshire Environment', packed with information, findings, statistics, graphs and policy statements in a very readable presentation. More than that, their conclusions and future intentions bode well for the years ahead, especially since government agencies and the voluntary watchdogs will be monitoring developments. Additional pairs-of-hands are always welcome on countryside management schemes.

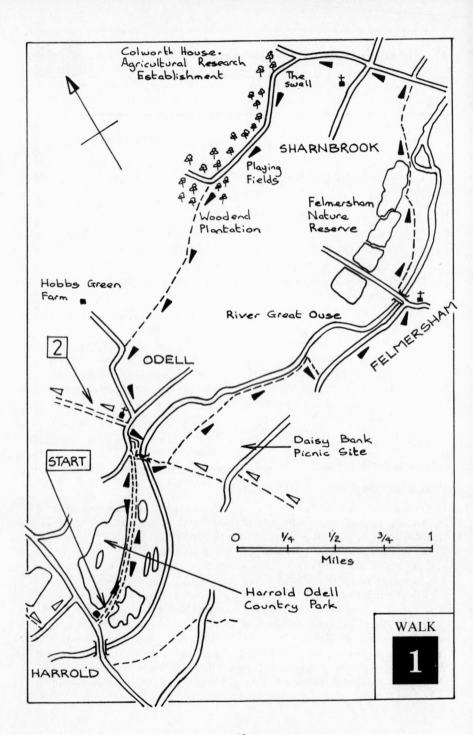

Colworth House.
Agricultural Research
Establishment

The Swell

SHARNBROOK

Playing Fields

Felmersham Nature Reserve

Woodend Plantation

Hobbs Green Farm

River Great Ouse

2

ODELL

FELMERSHAM

Daisy Bank Picnic Site

START

0   1/4   1/2   3/4   1
Miles

Harrold Odell Country Park

HARROLD

WALK

1

12

Of course, walkers don't have an unblemished track record in keeping the Country Code. Taking liberties on the farms by going onto private land for example, treading out wrong paths in crops (farmers should reconstitute paths after ploughing) and instances of being argumentative when advice is given. Farmers earn their livelihood from their lands and, whilst not all are 'lilywhite', they are the countryside custodians. It is not unknown for farmers to invite walkers in for a cup of tea and help them plan their routes!

After all, one does not have unlimited freedom to roam elsewhere – outsiders cannot go into factories or coal mines, for example. It's another matter where landowners forbid the use of certain footpaths, as in cases highlighted by the Ramblers' Association. Another factor is that one can by indiscriminate walking be spreading disease, even into the human chain. Dog owners, in the eyes of farmers, top the suspicion list, for dogs can wreak havoc if let loose amongst livestock.

WALK

HARROLD – ODELL – FELMERSHAM – SHARNBROOK

Leave the Visitors' Centre and car-park complex through the gates, down the broad gravel drive, laid by the Bedfordshire Ranger Service. Waters stretch out on both sides, providing nesting for many species of bird, particularly on the islands and the floating pontoons, out of harm's way. As with the Tring Reservoirs these are wonderful places for ornithologists. Green arrows on posts indicate the way.

In the park many plant species come into view – willow, teasels, rosebay willow herb, ragwort and a host more, so a handbook would be useful. Books on the park can be purchased from the Visitors' Centre. Encircled by an abundance of waterside plants is our second stretch of water, before we leave the park gate, then stroll through a small field planted with young trees – I always applaud tree schemes – into Horsefair Lane, Odell.

The pleasure of stone and thatch cottages in the villages of north Bedfordshire welcomes the visitor and here they are around the 'Bell' P.H., near the bend in the main road. Bear right down Mill Lane, but before rushing off take a good look at the renovated cottages just here – all credit for this sort of effort. Odell mill, privately owned, still retains its iron waterwheel and is, needless to say, in limestone under a slated roof pierced by dormer windows, all well refurbished. The paths are clear and a derelict sluice may be noticed on the approach to the footbridge over the River Great Ouse as it meanders its way toward Bedford.

Rivers are a fascination, so spare some time here. The unexpected quite often is seen. Then go foward for about 50 yards to where a stile bearing a yellow arrow must be discovered in the L.H. hedgerow which can

13

be almost overgrown and out of sight. Use your secateurs and help keep it open. Make for the top boundary in this riverside sheep meadow, walking beside a long bed of thistles wired off. Just visible and set amongst the trees on the other bank stands Odell Castle, of Norman origin, and basically of motte and bailey form.

Stay by the R.H., crossing stiles as they come, with reminders that this is the yellow arrow footpath route. For about ¾ mile the walk is at the riverside providing a good chance of seeing Canada Geese (now a resident bird) of the Anatidae family, 40″ in length full grown, having a distinctive black neck and head, white cheeks and light brown body.

Some nettles are likely in places by the waterside, though anglers make a way through most times in the season, and the stretch finishes on passing over a footbridge into the next meadow. Change of direction away from the river staying by the R.H. hedge up the slope of this sheep meadow, leaving by a stile in the corner and out onto the Felmersham road turning left. This unavoidable stretch of undulating road is made pleasant by the great amount of trees on each side affording views of Sharnbrook woods in the middle distance (part of the return leg of this walk).

Arriving at Felmersham Bridge there is a place set aside with seating commanding a fine river view, whilst behind stands the church on the rise, noted for its arcaded shaft front and the trefoil and quatrefoil headed windows looking down on the scene.

Over the bridge and enter the riverside meadow marked by a green arrow setting off in a N.E. direction, initially staying by the rush beds of the river bank. Then, after going through a gate, turn away from the river, walking between two barbed-wire fences, and with another change of direction we find outselves alongside a drainage watercourse which is crossed by a convenient bridge displaying a green arrow sign. The Felmersham lakes, once a series of gravel pits, lie behind the L.H. hedge; not surprisingly the whole area is now a nature reserve – the second in this walk.

Leave the end of the hedge, striking out on the bridleway in the direction of the windmill tower, and once there make for the grassy path on the R.H.S. of the garden on a clearly defined way. Gone are the sails though it still retains its ogee shaped green cap and instead it has been given an observation floor, a clock and chimes. Be careful, for in front is a road bend, so go left to walk the length of Sharnbrook High Street. Again this is a limestone village sporting many examples of proud-pointing between the mellowed freestones, though interspersed with red brickwork which is not entirely in keeping. Also, quite a lot of thatched roofs and a plentiful collection of leaded windows. So, all in all this is a pleasant village of vernacular interest. Part way along the High Street a side road for Harrold is seen, but continue on, having admired the splendid view of Sharnbrook church whose steeple is supported by flying buttresses and which has a noteworthy series of lancet windows in the fabric.

There is a risk of going down a wrong road on leaving the village so be careful. First pass the Souldrop turning on your right and continue past the Colworth House drive (a Unilever Research Centre), bungalows left and grounds across the road. This brings us out onto a 'tee' junction with a branch road for a lodge entrance; go forward into Yelnow Lane. (Ignore the sharp left turn at this junction).

The ash-lined rural road walk is no burden, and there is a school playing field acting as a diversion, as well as glimpses of the river valley. When the road bend is reached look out for the bridleway into the mixed wood belt of beech, ash, oak, sycamore and hazel and watch out for the yellow and green arrow markers. If you cannot see any you are lost! At the western wood boundary turn R. for about 50 yards and find the almost hidden stile taking the walker out into the field; this also has marker arrows.

A path follows the wood's edge, but our route is directly away such that the hedgerow is on our R.H.S. Full view of the Great Ouse valley, unless there is a mist, staying on the high ground. In time this becomes a firm track way with a turn off for Hobbs Green Farm becoming now a minor road; a row of cottages in various states of renovation are met on the bend, so don't hurry here, and on down the hollow road past the pinnacled, towered Odell church with its plain traceried glass windows.

Right at the road, and so on round into Horsefair Lane. Use the initial section of the drive up to the Country Park gate, but this time turn off R. inside the Park and walk around the large expanse of water in an anti-clockwise manner. Thus we get a different aspect of the scenery with riverside trees as a backdrop; there is an island in the middle so birds can be assured, and it goes without saying that binoculars should be essential equipment.

Along the boundary road is a coniferous tree-belt containing a path, thus proving an alternative ending to the walk, and you will observe numbers of picnic tables around the water's perimeter. As a bonus there is a second chance to look around the Visitors' Centre and its particularly good set of pictures and notes on the bird species and fauna of the area.

Conservation and the Diminishing Countryside

Places included: HARROLD – ODELL.

Length of walk: 6¼ miles.

Grid Ref: Sheet 153 956 566.

Parking: Harrold Odell Country Park car park.

Bus services: 133, 134, 135 and 136.

Public Houses: The Bell (Odell), The Mad Dog (Little Odell) and pubs in Harrold.

Walk Links: Walks 1, 2 and 3 all start from the Visitors' Centre car park.

Notes 1: Harrold is one of Bedfordshire's limestone villages with two places of interest on its gem of a tree-fringed village green. One is the famous circular lock-up of 1824 vintage and the other is an open-pillared stallholders' market.

2. The bridge over the River Great Ouse with sections dating from the 12th century can be counted as Harrold's other noteworthy structure, used on Walk 3.

3: See Note for Walk 1.

CONSERVATION AND THE DIMINISHING COUNTRYSIDE

Except for articles in the 'quality' newspapers and the occasional piece in local newspapers pleading for a reprieve for some countryside or discussing a land controversy, little gets written on this subject.

Firstly towns and their industrial areas invariably mean an irreversible occupation of land and hence the policy of 'infilling' building and urban renewal where possible. Unfortunately much virgin land is also being taken for house building. Gone are the days when whole villages decayed, disappearing into fields to await rediscovery (see deserted villages in Book 1); these days they are just absorbed into suburbs.

The second utilisation of land in this highly mobile age brings us to transportation provisions, with motorways, by-passes and airports all making encroachments. Canals make no demands, having as it were become part of the scenery, and with the railway network now much diminished many tracks have become rural walks, e.g. the Stevington Country Walk. The exception for railways in our day comes in the form of the controversial Channel Tunnel Link.

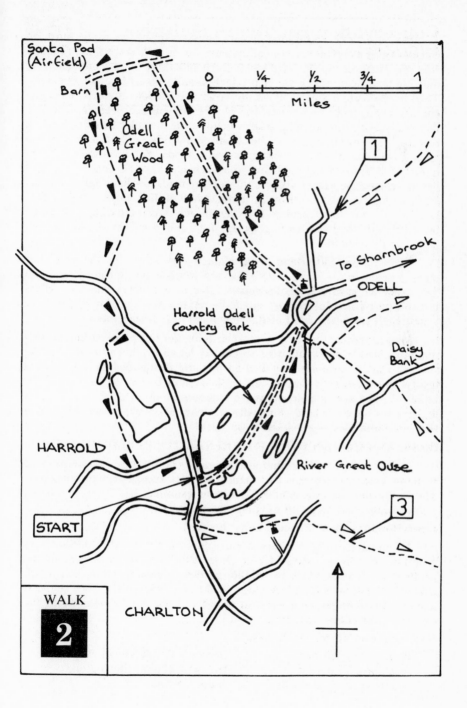

Santa Pod
(Airfield)

Barn

Odell
Great
Wood

0   ¼   ½   ¾   1
Miles

1

To Sharnbrook

ODELL

Harrold Odell
Country Park

Daisy
Bank

HARROLD

River Great Ouse

3

START

WALK
2

CHARLTON

Whatever our rose-tinted glasses might suggest, farming must be considered as a capital investment industry for its cash crops and products. However, with European surpluses in foodstuffs there's every indication we may see land being taken out of production and utilised in other manners. This diversification will likely as not enter less obvious areas of specialist cheeses, exotic fruits and vegetables. More mono-cultures seem a possibility in this diversification, examples of which are the lavender fields of Norfolk or the bulb-growing areas of Lincolnshire. Already in Norfolk this movement has commenced, decreasing its arable lands. For instance at Thornham Parva some of the fields and the parkland have become community based, serving the nearby villages with nature trails, a village hall, a schools study centre, a garden centre in a redundant walled garden and artists/craftsmen/renovators earning a living in the farm buildings, plus the inevitable gift shop-cum-café. Even the local pub has been drawn into an activities programme.

I can foresee more land being planted with trees, for the trend has already begun in the north, where the tendency is to go for coniferous types for a quicker cash return. Especially after recent storm damage, where possible native deciduous types should be set, not maturing for 100 or more years. Let's hope that most of the remaining hedges stay intact.

Man cannot be said to be a good custodian of this planet, often putting mammon first. Conservationists would say let nature have her land back; she will always recolonise, as disused pits and dismantled railways would testify. The message is happily getting through to Fords, the Dagenham car builders; they are bringing massive amounts of top soil, creating a new topography on waste land along with stretches of water. Fords are pleased that coots and herons recognise their work!

BEDS. AND CAMBS. WILDLIFE TRUST SITES IN BEDFORDSHIRE

It may not be realised that all England's counties are in a network of Wildlife Trusts which own and manage sites of special scientific interest. The Beds. and Cambs. Wildlife Trust, for example, has 18 or so sites in Bedfordshire with about 19 in Huntingdonshire.

Priory Country Park, Barkers Lane, Bedford.

Headquarters and Visitors' Centre for the Trust, with 200 acres of grounds close by the River Great Ouse, 80 of which are water. In the grounds are nature trails, a wildlife garden, a new meadow and a full perimeter walk around Priory Lake. Within 1½ miles of the town centre it aims to stimulate public interest in wildlife, at the same time catering for canoeing and sailing activities.

Beds. and Cambs. managed sites:-

Wymington Meadow.	Begwary Brook Marsh, Wyboston.
Sharnbrook Summit.	Holywell Marsh, Stevington.
Felmersham Gravel Pits.	Judge's Spinney, Oakley.

Cople Pits.

Millbrook Pillinge.

Old Warden Tunnel.

Cooper's Hill, Ampthill.

Sandy Banks, Clophill.

Flitwick Moor.

Arlesey Old Moat.

Kings Wood, Heath and Reach.

Dropshort Marsh, Toddington.

Sewell Cutting.

Totternhoe Knolls.

Many of these sites are open to the public, though others can only be visited by members either in conducted parties or with restricted access. These places, many of them S.S.S.I.s, require working parties for scrub clearance etc., so that their special features can be retained. Natural history notes in this book come from site brochures supplied by the Trust.

Why not join them and do something for Bedfordshire's countryside?

WALK

2

HARROLD – ODELL

The first stage of this particular walk is the same as the previous Odell and Harrold Country Park start, in that the main thoroughfare across the park is used and out into Odell via Horsefair Lane. Join the road by 'The Bell' P.H. and set off in the direction of Sharnbrook, then not far beyond the first bend and before Odell church enter the bridleway left across the road. This is a tree-lined avenue, having broad swathes of grass on each side, and we are now following green arrow markers. Two gates are passed through and we find recent plantings of beech, chestnuts and poplars.

One cannot but be impressed by the magnificence of Odell Great Wood, but be warned that it can be quite damp or muddy underfoot, as the blue damsel flies testify in summer months. Ahead we take the broad clearway into the wood (green arrowed). In places, especially near the southern side, brushwood and undercover are being cleared under management schemes, opening up the woodland floor, but the visitor must on no account stray from the main drive and dogs must be kept on leads. The reason being that this habitat is of great environmental importance. Silver-leaf, vetches, cow-parsley, bluebells, sorrells, sedges and varieties of grasses can be seen, but also keep a lookout for bird, mammal and insect life. As will be discovered the wood has a considerable diversity in its mixed deciduous trees – no wonder it is a Site of Special Scientific Interest.

Mid-way, eight paths cross over and our way is forward on a narrower, even muddier green path; eventually the wood's edge is reached, keep onward in the field until coming across a bridleway crossing at the end of a R.H. tree-belt. Here is the boundary of the Santa Pod Raceway, well-known for the drag car competitions, and in fact by going forward just a bit more the course and buildings can be clearly seen in the distance. (The redundant dispersal boundary road still exists right in front of you, for this was once the Podington WWII airfield – Pod in Santa Pod is of course Podington).

Left at the bridleway crossing, taking us into the apron area of a hangar and it is important to seek out the bridleway exit situated at the rear of this hangar. Though very overgrown with nettle banks the original path exists alongside and is given arrow markers. Behind the hangar we are in the wood again, which is after all, the highlight of the walk, on very clayey soil; water-loving plants and grasses thrive in the damp soil. The bridleway leaves the wood becoming an enjoyable broad green lane beside Odell Great Wood; from here the walker looks out to other pockets of woodland across the arable fields on this relatively high ground above the river valley.

After a further ½ mile the bridleway breaks away from the wood's edge, becoming a broad tree-lined lane slowly descending down the contours and terminating on the Harrold road. (Hinwick is in the other direction). Turn towards Harrold for a short road walk, then when five bungalows come into view find the F.P. sign by them, almost hidden under the spread of the trees here.

Cross this field to the far hedge, then turn left once over the stile, joining the narrow path bounded by a fence on your left and a babbling brook under a hedgerow; birds fly up and down this natural corridor searching for food. Nettles are a hazard again and beware of the barbed-wire. Another stile is encountered leading toward Harrold's northern lake which is only seen for a short time; here binoculars are useful for those with naturalist inclinations. The path diverts through a hedge out into a long meadow, hiding the waters; stay by the L.H. boundary. A grassy lane is entered from the end stile, close by a timber saw-mill, and a last sighting of the lake is made; now aim for Harrold by means of a grass path by a paddock, (don't divert right).

This leads you up to a brook between a house and a long stone wall. Go across the footbridge, then on gaining the path on the other side turn right (westward), then on reaching house 68A (on your right) go left through a gap and this drive brings you out in front of Harrold Green Garage.

The tree-lined green with its famous circular lock-up, thatched cottages, 1847 school and octagonal-roofed open market building just cannot be ignored, whatever the weather. A visually satisfying composition.

Continue down the High Street in front of the garage (eastwards) and so up to the tee junction. Those fascinated by houses of all shapes and ages – and I am one – will not find this stretch boring. And so into the Country Park and I would suggest taking the path in the pine trees for the return to the Visitors' Centre.

Bedfordshire and all the Shires

Places included: HARROLD – OUTSKIRTS OF CARLTON AND PAVENHAM – ODELL

Walk length: 5¾ miles.

Grid Ref: Sheet 153 956 566.

Parking: Harrold Odell Country Park car park.

Bus services: 133, 134, 135 and 136.

Public Houses: The Fox (Carlton) and pubs in Harrold. The Bell (Odell).

Walk Links: Walks 1, 2 and 3 all start from the Visitors' Centre car park.

This walk can be connected with Walk 25 for Stevington using bridleways through Pavenham and the riverside path, which is a lovely area.

Notes 1: The Bedfordshire C.C. Picnic Site on the Carlton-Felmersham road, named Daisy Bank, makes a good stopping place overlooking the river.

2: Carlton village close by Harrold should be visited.

BEFORDSHIRE AND ALL THE OTHER SHIRES

For more than 400 years the counties of England performed their functions. They were first recorded on maps by Christopher Saxton who, after nine years surveying on horseback, produced his series of county maps in 1570. Some counties had sub-divisions; Yorkshire with three Ridings (a riding is a third); Lincoln had Lindsey, Kesteven and Holland, whilst Suffolk and Surrey were big enough to have an East and West.

Then came an April Fool's trick with a vengeance, for on April 1st 1974 several counties were swept away altogether and great administration areas were carved out of the original counties, all resulting from the Boundary Commission's findings of 1970-72. The White Paper writing on county sentiments said that "they would not be outraged", then on a conciliatory note the then Minister of the Environment stated "the new counties were created for statutory purposes" and "people were at liberty to refer to their traditional county names".

The new non-county names include Cumbria, West Midlands, Avon, Humberside, Cleveland, Tyne and Wear, Merseyside and a few others;

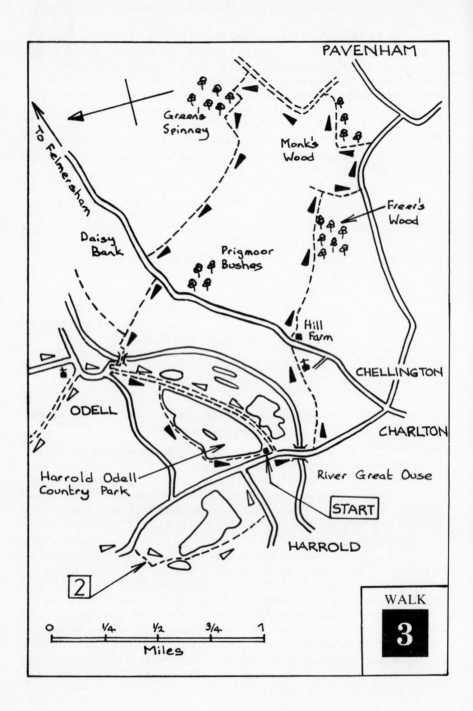

PAVENHAM

To Felmersham

Green's
Spinney

Monk's
Wood

Freel's
Wood

Daisy
Bank

Prigmoor
Bushes

Hill
Farm

CHELLINGTON

ODELL

CHARLTON

Harrold Odell
Country Park

River Great Ouse

START

HARROLD

2

WALK
3

0   ¼   ½   ¾   1
Miles

rivers are so convenient for naming. Herefordshire and Worcestershire were brought together at the altar in a shotgun marriage, then there is the instance of Rutland going into Leicestershire but still keeping its identity. By the way, think of all the counties and place names that include -cester, -chester or -caister or something similar showing Roman connections – nineteen hundred years of history were being disrupted in just four years. Our English roots are a coalescence of Celtic, Gaelic, Saxon, Roman, Danish, Angles and Norman strands among others.

County allegiance showed up in those times of change, for Yorkshire, that giant of English counties, "died in its sleep" proclaimed the 'Yorkshire Post'. But Yorkshire did not die; it split into North, South and West with chunks taken out on the coasts. If Yorkshire's entity could be tumbled, Bedfordshire could well have been forced into a marriage with Northamptonshire or Huntingdonshire. At that time in the 1970s these changes proved the most drastic ever in the history of local government, though some subsequent big upheavals greatly affected the conurbation County Councils.

"Don't be brainwashed into thinking there has been any change at all in the geographical, ancient and traditional counties of England – there hasn't" say the writers in 'This England'. Regularly seen on the magazine shelves of newsagents and so popular with those living away from the mother country, this publication is in the vanguard of the re-recognition of all our traditional counties. They launched the 'Save Our Shires' campaign and say in our case "Stay loyal to the traditional county of Bedfordshire".

WALK

HARROLD – OUTSKIRTS OF CARLTON AND PAVENHAM – ODELL

3

Leave the Country Park and cross Harrold Bridge, overlooking a spillway on the Bedford side of the river. Then, on leaving the bridge with its walkers' refuges and before the path continues on a raised causeway above the 3' flood level marker, cross the road to the F.P. sign in the gateway. Now the walk proper starts, crossing the field making for a cleft in the opposite hedge below the church profile in a direction away from the river. There on the stile a yellow arrow acts as an indicator, and the next rising section can be sticky in wet weather being a cow-trail between fields. On the hilltop grand views over the Country Park are gained, then skirting the adjacent church stay by the remnant hedgerow in this field making for the L.H.E. of the roadside farm buildings.

Cross the road to the F.P. sign, going down an area beside a steel constructed grain barn, then over a gate bearing another yellow arrow before entering an arable field. Behind Hill Farm one finds what appears to be a 'hollow-way', so cross a wire there on the edge and proceed along the top of the L.H. bank, confirmed part way by a stile on this footpath. Meadow flowers grow through here, but so do nettles and thistles, then we

23

find the path veers slightly left making for the L.H.E. of Freer's Wood. On the approach pockets of water-loving grasses grow, showing this constitutes the run-off conditions of the high ground here.

The going now becomes a dirt track beside the dense woodland, punctuated by the derelict form of Freer's Wood Farm where nature has set about reclaiming her stones and mortar. Continue up to the 'tee' B.W. junction, where we turn right on the stoney track, crossing the field and arriving on the Carlton-Pavenham road. L. now for a short distance, then when the road descends look out for the B.W. sign and green arrow in the roadside hedgerow gap. This leads up to a field gate after passing through a pocket of trees. Shut the gate and go A.C.W. beside the trees of Monk's Wood coming upon a field access track from West End Farm. Change into a northerly direction on this track uphill, which bears right becoming a ridge walk. Pavenham church can clearly be seen against the trees in the middle distance over in the east.

Carry on until the bridleway peters out abruptly at a field corner; in this vicinity the Pavenham link comes up crossing the ditch by a two-plank bridge. At this point there will be a hedge running across left to the neighbouring spinney, so turn in front of the row and walk with it on your R.H.S. There may or may not be a clear path, but on gaining the spinney stay in this field and go round the L.H.E. of the wood. Look for a gap in the hedge and carefully tread over the wires there. Keeping on the wood boundary continue on past, coming upon a track junction. The rest is easy and downhill with splendid views across the Gt. Ouse valley (the reason for doing the walk in an anti-clockwise direction).

Heading for Odell now on a very wide grass track which clips the end of a treeline, gaining super views. Five churches can be seen on the slope down to the road – try identifying them on an O.S. map. The landscape can only be described as vast and memorable. Bedfordshire's Daisy Bank picnic site is just along the Felmersham road a short distance if you want a stop with a vantage position.

Dog-leg left on the road to the B.W. sign green arrowed. A rough track brings us up to a warning about dog control and sheep hazards at a field gateway. Message taken, go direct to the bridge near a weir. Cross our now familiar river going towards the well-restored Odell mill retaining its iron wheel; the mill leet here bounds the garden of 'The Bell' P.H. Stone cottages in Mill Lane received loving care in their revival now lending, as they write in some guide books, local colour.

Close by 'The Bell' P.H. in Odell – a village appearing in several of these walks – one finds Horsefair Lane leading to the perimeter of the Country Park, where we have a choice. Either go forward on the broad gravel path between the waters or use the footpath on the northern side of the water. In this alternative one has greater opportunity for observing the birdlife and the added scenic advantage of having the willows as a backdrop growing between the lakes and the river. Chances are you will be this way again on another walk.

Bedfordshire Sayings

Places included: RISELEY

Length of walk: 6½ miles.

Grid Ref: Sheet 153 039 631.

Parking: In the vicinity of the church turning R. of School Road.

Bus Services: 152.

Public Houses: The Fox and Hounds also Five Bells (both in Riseley).

Walks Links: The Knotting – Melchbourne road connects with Walk 5 and using Coppice Wood bridleway and country roads the return of Walk 6 is met.The Riseley to Bletsoe road makes contact with Walk 7 from Thurleigh.

BEDFORDSHIRE SAYINGS

I doubt if anyone would deny that our grandparents had a richer range of phrases than the present generation. These days we are not renowned for our appetite for reading, whilst we do a lot of T.V. watching, whence come our catch phrases. The oral tradition of our forebears could sum up all situations in a succinct manner and let their views be known overtly or indirectly bringing in all aspects of living. These sayings, now fast disappearing, displayed great sagacity and commonsense; what is more in the days of few pictures an apt choice of words could convey visual impressions to the hearers for all human moods.

Sayings included here come from oral sources, Bedfordshire books and inscriptions on lacemaking bobbins. Love, relations, sayings of every description and 'outside' news are to be found e.g. 'Trafalgar Victory' news brought into the village by the lace dealers and itinerant salesmen.

Unless necessary, interpretations for the sayings are not given.

It's black over Will's mother's.

Better do well late than never.

As bent as a nine bob note. (Only ten and twenty shillings bank notes were in general usage).

Where true love is planted it grows.

Never faint.

Do not be forgetful.

Time is short.

If I am ragged my heart is true.

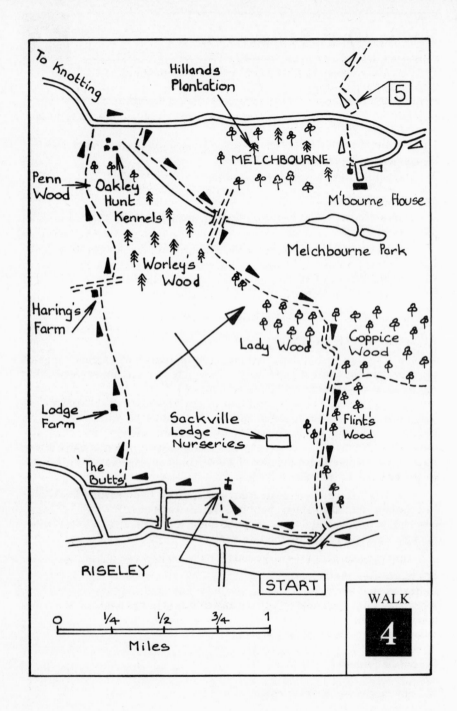

To Knotting

Hillands Plantation

5

MELCHBOURNE

Penn Wood

Oakley Hunt Kennels

M'bourne House

Melchbourne Park

Worley's Wood

Haring's Farm

Lady Wood

Coppice Wood

Flint's Wood

Lodge Farm

Sackville Lodge Nurseries

The Butts

RISELEY

START

0   ¼   ½   ¾   1
Miles

WALK
4

26

Apples always go to where there are orchards.
Keep your temper.
While you are awake you have got to think of something.
Love is a sharp thorn.
Wait for the waggon.
As plain as Dunstable road. (The broad coach road to London, totally uninteresting, 1858).
Those were the days when plait went well. (Good income from making Dunstable plait.)
As crooked as Crawley brook. (The nameless brook rising near Woburn that flows by Crawley, meandering 80 miles instead of the straight 18 miles to join the R. Gt. Ouse, 1858).
The Bailiff of Bedford is coming. (A warning that best get your cattle into safety in winter time, for sudden rains would make the R. Gt. Ouse swollen and flood and you ran the risk of the Bailiff of Bedford impounding your cows, 1858).
Before you could say knife.
Let the dog see the rabbit.

WALK

RISELEY

After parking near Riseley church walk back down Church Lane, then rounding the corner R. continue into Rotten Row still amongst the houses; as a curiosity an old windlass well is passed on the way. The last house is called 'The Bungalow', having a white paling fence, and the road straightens out called 'The Butts' on the maps.

Right now into the Lodge Farm drive, planted out with young trees which will be effective in years to come. Don't use the drive, but stay on the grass verge alongside the R.H. field, bearing away from the farm buildings which are private, and up to a side hedgerow. The way forward passes on the right side of red brick outbuildings at the pole-mounted power-cable junction. Melchbourne Park forms the skyline and it is good to see the hedgerows retained. At the end of the barns pass over the track and into the next field, staying on the L.H.S. of the hedgerow with a line of pole-mounted power-cables. This stretch becomes a causeway between fields, possibly an old hedgerow bank. All around we savour the giant scale of gentle, undulating mixed Bedfordshire landscape, interspersed only by farm buildings. Pass a cottage and up to Harings Farm drive, lined by maturing trees – be careful you don't tread on any guinea fowl! Leave, bearing right on the right of way.

Don't go up to Worley Wood but take the B.W. left, gaining good views again, but it can be exposed and windy. No possibility of getting lost, but the way does change around quite a bit and we pass through a recently cleared green lane now in excellent condition. Penn Wood beside us now, walking in the open fields, so out onto the Knotting/Melchbourne road. There are teazels to be seen; these heads as most will know were used for raising nap on freshly woven cloth; they are a curious plant usually signifying the presence of water.

A road walk for a bit, still on a clockwise circular, past the brick built Oakley Hunt Kennels and likely as not the hounds will detect you and give a rousing welcome; they can be seen in the compounds and paddocks.

And now comes the tricky section, for the footpath and bridleway used are ploughed out, so just keep to the description. Where the road bears slightly left enter the field at the access and follow the remnant hedgeline towards Worley Wood. (The kennels are on the other side of this field). When you see two fields to go before getting to the wood go left into the long field which could contain rape seed or an arable crop and be on the R.H.S. of the hedge, (your left). One has quite honestly just got to push through, so now this walk is written down the farmer might be kind enough to leave a walking strip. For when you do get to the other end use a short section of good country bridleway. You can see what can easily happen; the whole bridleway turned over to crops. Unless you are an experienced walker and can use a compass you could not begin to tackle the myriad lost footpaths in Bedfordshire using 1:25,000 scale maps. Having said all that, let's get on with the walk assuming you have got to the right place by going parallel with Worley Wood.

Beside a small wood pocket containing a pond and stream which turn out to be the headwaters of Melchbourne Park lake (bourne, bourn or born signifies a stream). Go right around the wood pocket on the roving bridge taking a substantial B.W. up to the corner of Worley Wood. Several tracks and footpaths converge in these quarters, at least they do on the O.S. map, and another pond is found being systematically filled in – the third seen on this walk and we are still rising onto a flat area. And now watch carefully again. Although marked as a B.W. and used by riders, a path between two fields leaves Worley Wood, goes alongside a ditch and odd remaining trees, making for the L.H.E. of Lady Wood ahead. Rough going but passable. Melchbourne House from up here displays better proportions that when seen on the village side.

For a short section by Lady Wood keep your eye open for a walker's gate at the juncture with Coppice Wood, distinguished by a narrow joining tree belt. This can be missed. Go through the open neck of woodland, the path being marked out by green footpath notices, and meet the concrete throughway. Make for the southern side of Coppice Wood where a concrete road will be found – more signs of the military in N. Bedfordshire. Interestingly there's some tree colonising naturally by the roadside, seeded no doubt from the Coppice Wood close by, and this becomes our way for the next stretch. The concrete side 'pads' could have served for military vehicles or dispersal aircraft in wartime, being not that far from Thurleigh.

The atmosphere of a country road pervades the stretch as we go through the area known as Flint's Wood; certain areas are planted out with limes growing in straight rows, all making for variety in this walk – a good deal of wooded stretches compared with other walks in the book. Two gates are passed through and the entrance for Sackville Nurseries found on our right as we walk the wooded road down to the Riseley road by the Lodge gates. Walk toward Riseley but not too far, keeping a look out for a gap in the side hedge which leads you back into the fields over a footbridge, re-crossing the river at the Lodge gates. We now pass through a series of small fields on a path sometimes bounded by an electric fence and close by the river along the backs of the houses. There's livestock grazing, so keep a lookout as to where they are; stiles and plank bridges mark the way. Before long the church comes clearly into view and an unmistakable broad way rising up the slope to the churchyard wall. By following left and through the gap in the corner of this field make your way round to the front entrance of the church.

Bedfordshire Agriculture and Horticulture

Places included: MELCHBOURNE – YELDEN

Length of walk: 6½ miles.

Grid Ref: Sheet 153 029 654.

Parking: Turn into village and park near church, keeping clear of the bend on the approach to Melchbourne House.

Bus services: Nil.

Public Houses: St. John's Arms (Melchbourne) and The Chequers (Yelden).

Walk Links: Access for Walk 4 can be gained on the Knotting road. Bridleway from northeast side of this walk and road takes you into Upper Dean for Walk 6.

Notes 1: Impressive motte and bailey earthworks of the Trailly's family fortification circa 1300, ruined later that century, makes a good photographic subject.

2: Following the River Til an extension can be made into the photogenic hamlet of Shelton.

3: Melchbourne has a continuous row of eight thatched cottages near the church, all with different front doors and varying front gardens; the fine towered church has clear glass windows in the Georgian round-head manner. To this writer Melchbourne House presents an unharmonious composition marred by the sash windows not being in accordance with the 'golden ratio'

BEDFORDSHIRE AGRICULTURE AND HORTICULTURE

Of Bedfordshire's approx. 125,000 hectares (approx. 300,000 acres) – hectares is the usual unit of area measure these days – half the farm land in the county has the highest classifications, those of Grades 1 and 2 agricultural land. These lie between the classical grain belt of East Anglia and the mixed farming of the Midlands.

Arable crops account for most of the land in the county under cultivation, with the heavy traditional wheat-growing land in the north. Since the 1970s when Britain joined the E.E.C., cereals and oilseed rape production saw a big increase in output. This increase has been to some extent at the expense of Bedfordshire's traditional field-scale vegetable

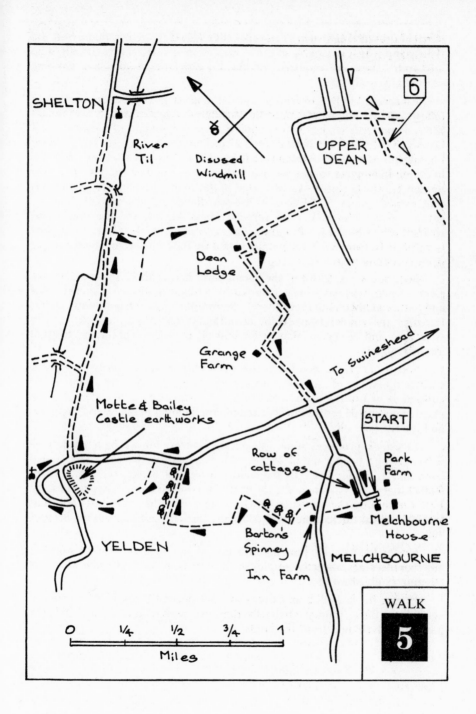

SHELTON

River Til

Disused Windmill

6

UPPER DEAN

Dean Lodge

Grange Farm

To Swineshead

START

Park Farm

Motte & Bailey Castle earthworks

Row of cottages

Melchbourne House

YELDEN

Barton's Spinney

MELCHBOURNE

Inn Farm

0   1/4   1/2   3/4   1
Miles

WALK

5

horticulture although such crops are still extensively grown mainly on the Greensand which is capable of growing early crops. However, considerable husbandry skills are required for keeping the land in good heart, being susceptible to drought.

An account of Bedfordshire's agricultural scene may be summarised as follows, though the figures must be considered a generalisation for the late 1980s as patterns change rather rapidly. For conversions, 1 hectare = 2.4 acres and there are 266 hectares in a square mile (104 hectares for a square kilometre). Also, bear in mind that the grids on Ordnance Survey maps are in fact in kilometres so you are using kilometres whether you like it or not. So now for the hectares:- Land rented in the county amounts to 38,000 and that owned comes to 54,000, whilst woodland on agricultural holdings covers 1,600 hectares. For the cereals, wheat 40,000, and the winter and spring barleys total 14,700; figures for oats not available. Oilseed rape has nearly 8,000, there's 850 for potatoes, and we have an area of 580 for sugar beet, representing the root crops.

For vegetables grown in the open nearly half of the 2,750 hectares are given over to Brussel sprouts, followed by cabbage at 455; next come onions and lettuce at about 180 each; there's cauliflower and beetroot jointly on 90. Parsnips and runner beans come near the 50 mark with peas, calabrese, sweetcorn and celery, in that order and all the other vegetables in quite minor amounts.

Soft fruits are headed by strawberries (43), then raspberries (19), also smaller quantities of currants and gooseberries are cultivated. Flowers for cutting, grown in the open, account for 44, whilst the area under glass or plastic takes up 55 for tomatoes, cucumbers, bedding plants, sweet peppers, and the list goes on.

Livestock produces some interesting figures, for we have cattle and calves giving a head count of 24,500 animals, of which there are 5,100 dairy cows and 1,750 for beef. In the county a total of 62,000 for pigs, nearly 60,000 sheep and lambs; goats, the other four-footed animal, approximately 190. Continuing the statistics, fowl for eggs and the table just less than 800,000, whilst ducks number 2,000 plus, last and not least, geese around 900.

On the head count, humans this time, 4,500 farmers, regular workers and partners are directly employed on the land in 1,350 holdings and farming establishments.

Horses for breeding and livery are not normally included in farming agriculture data, though obviously they are present and earn their own particular livelihood from the land.

MELCHBOURNE – YELDEN

A gravel drive leaves the church bend between Hillend Cottage and the Old School House but don't go too far, for the path used is behind the Old School House side fence and the hedge on the boundary of the next property. The grass path enters a field and the direction is against the R.H. hedge on the headlands. A pile of bricks in a ditch serves as a bridge out onto the road by the F.P. sign.

Alongside the neat Inn Farm – better proportioned than Melchbourne House considering this is a working farm vernacular building – is a substantial brick farmyard, beside which the footpath passes. Now on an excellent stone farm drive, it dog-legs to the woodline and stays close by the trees and rounds the corner of Barton's Spinney. There is another small dog-leg at the end of the Spinney, so make sure you go in a northerly direction ignoring the L.H. track. Cross the stream/pond on the farm bridge and proceed slightly upwards into Bedfordshire's cereal producing fields of which we see a lot in these walks north of Bedford. There comes a sharp L-turn between fields which are not big by comparison with South and East Bedfordshire. For although the countryside cannot be decribed as spectacular, there's sufficient interest in, for example, the varied field shapes augmented by the trees and undulations. So on past the archetypal red brick Crowfield Farm and strike out across the field behind the farm if there is not a path. This path was literally ploughed up before my eyes when walking here, so it is up to ramblers to keep these and other paths open.

When across the field there, you will find a narrow headland by a high double hedge; go right in a north-easterly direction onto the Swineshead/Yelden road, Melchbourne House in good view from this position. Left in the direction of Yelden, as the bridleway intended for use has now completely gone, then after about 300 yards enter the field on your left at the broken gateway. Stay with the R.H. hedge and it can be very awkward as the headland gets ploughed-out and there is a ditch very close by with a risk of falling in. Round the corner, being careful with your footing and before long the hedge gives way to a fence dividing a sheep pasture and some very notable earthworks. Yelden church, with its rather stumpy spire, appears over the roof-line of the village, whilst on the skyline we see the array of aerials of a wireless station.

Enter the sheep meadow by the stile and make for the church, gaining the village road close by a field pond. There is no mistaking the motte and bailey earthworks here, enclosed by extensive multiple ditches and barbicans. In fact, as an alternative, you can walk by the earthworks, so enabling exploration and photography.

But I would recommend a short diversion round Yelden, looking at the houses before going up to the church along Spring Lane returning onto this outing via Church Lane. (Spring as in water, I would suspect; you will see why). We leave the remains of the de Trailly's castle that's been in a ruinous state for over six centuries, and make use of the minor road on the main bend in the direction of Bottom Farm. On the one side is a drainage channel now set out with young sycamores and willows that will enhance this corner. There is a derelict farmyard nearby, but in a few moments compare the buildings on each side, one in the indigenous stone and thatch contrasted with the villa built on high ground in a hacienda style and landscaped down to the pond.

We find ourselves on a concrete road running out into the fields, but this turns toward Middle Lodge. Go on at the B.W. sign on a rolled surfaced track feeling better on the feet, then cross over the track junction into an ash-lined green lane. Here nature is doing its best to take over, but since it is used by farm vehicles and riders the way stays open. The water-carrying ditch on the other side of the L. hedge maps show as the R. Til on its way to Tilbrook. Our next turning is onto a bridleway which can be seen from a gap in the R.H. hedgerow after about ¾ mile crossing a big field. (If this gap is missed and you reach the bridge over the R. Til then just turn about and keep a lookout on your left).

Looking back left gives us a sighting of Shelton hamlet, marked by the squat church tower in the spread of trees. Make for the substantial track coming up from the right which provides the way for crossing the hill top, and there are good tracks from now onwards. The sad form of Upper Dean windmill, a cracked tower with just two surviving arms, can also be observed and good views of north Bedfordshire commanded. This easy going track makes a turn south to the derelict Dean Lodge Farm with the 'bare bones' of its rafters on view – even the rear catslide wash-house. Here we turn right around the old farmsteading, there's a track left, which we don't use, going to Upper Dean, the link with Walk 6. Round the corner and Melchbourne House comes back into view before us, joining the gravel track beside a high sheltering hedge now on your left. The track makes a turn at a field corner copse and Grange Farm is approached. Another change of direction again going across the apron area of the farm, not forward, and walk along a drive road on to the road tee junction. On the other corner stands the St. John's Arms P.H. bearing a coronet above an 'S' in stone on the facade. Continue on this, the Knotting road, then on the bend after a little downhill stretch, turn into Park Road, marked village only. Everyone remarks upon the continuous terrace of eight thatched cottages, some with flowers in the front gardens, others with vegetables and some left for Mother Nature to do the cultivating.

Bedfordshire Landscape – a Sketch

Places included: SWINESHEAD – UPPER DEAN

Length of walk: 6 miles.

Grid Ref: Sheet 153 058 659.

Parking: In the lane near the church, without causing obstruction.

Bus services: 152 (Cedar).

Public Houses: Five Bells (Swineshead) and Prince of Wales (Upper Dean).

Walks Links: The road past the Prince of Wales P.H. and the next bridleway meets Walk 5, or Walk 5 can be joined on the Swineshead to Yelden road. Using the Riseley road on the south turning of the walk and the edge of Coppice Wood leads onto Walk 4.

Notes 1: The church with a very high tower and spire commands attention, deserving a closer look both for its external decoration and internal features.

BEDFORDSHIRE LANDSCAPE – A SKETCH

The county measures 33 miles from Studham in the south to Shelton in the north, and 21 miles from west of Harrold to Wrestlingworth in the east, making an area of 123,500 hectares (305,000 acres), broadly divided into urbanised 10%, farmland 77% (80% of which is arable), woodland 4%, mineral workings 1%, water undertakings 2.5%, and the remainder includes unfarmed land, disused railways etc. amounting to 5.5%.

Between the years from 1950 to the mid-1980s the population of Bedfordshire rose from 310,000 to 650,000, and in that time a tenth of the farmland was lost to building development and mineral workings. Nearly a third of the hedgerows were lost and some 10% of the woodland cleared, resulting in extensive losses of flora, while in addition 90% of the county's ponds have gone since 1902.

Bedfordshire is in fact one of the driest counties in Gt. Britain with an average rainfall of 24″ and a temperature range of 17°C in July to 4°C typically for February. A wide range of geological stratas in the county provide a major influence on the topography and land usage, and to the north west deposits of Gt. Oolite yield stone of building quality, to the north of Ampthill lie the Oxford Clay beds – source of the brick making industry –

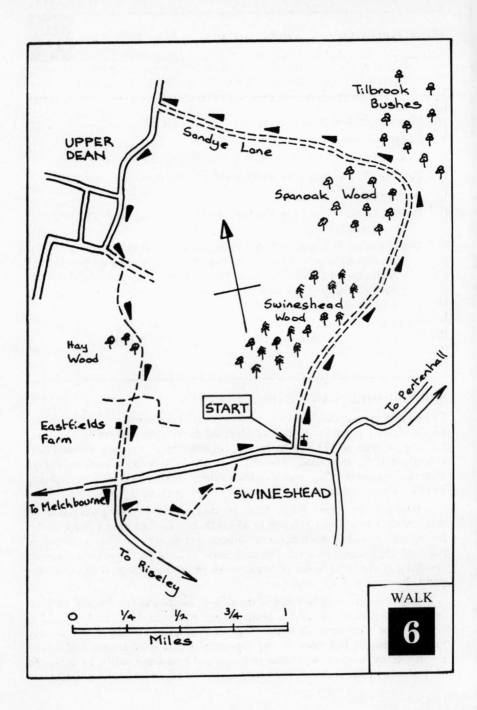

Tilbrook Bushes

Sandye Lane

UPPER DEAN

Spanoak Wood

Swineshead Wood

Hay Wood

Eastfields Farm

START

To Partenhall

To Melchbourne

SWINESHEAD

To Riseley

0   ¼   ½   ¾   1

Miles

WALK

6

whilst in the River Gt. Ouse valley and the River Ivel the gravels gave rise to considerable quarrying. In these valleys one finds the alluvial soils, whilst in the middle of the county lying in a north-easterly direction is the renowned Lower Greensand ridge. Immediately to the south the area consists mainly of Gault Clay, then at the southern end of the county are the familiar chalk hills of the Chilterns. These gave rise to whiting, lime and cement industries, all but a shadow of their former selves. Also to be noted was the drift working for Totternhoe stone, having extensive usage as a material for church interiors and as a lining stone in many of the cellars in the Dunstable area.

Agricultural land throughout falls into the first three grades of quality in a scale of five as determined by the Ministry of Agriculture and Fisheries, making this one of the best agricultural counties in the country. Walking north of Bedford the arable nature of the countryside becomes very apparent. The arable characteristic of the county has undergone a steady change in recent times with the widespread loss of hedgerows and trees; also much of the permanent pasture has been converted into cereal production. Oilseed rape introduced now on a considerable scale turns the landscape into a vivid yellow in the springtime, whilst on the horticultural scene the hardy 'Bedfordshire' brussel sprout, because of its late maturing, fits into labour requirements after the potato and sugar beet harvests – a horticultural industry founded on the usage of cheap stable manure brought out of London.

Woodland cover was in steady decrease but fortunately in the last few years the policies of private owners, the county and the Forestry Commission have meant substantial increase in the planting programmes.

WALK

6

SWINESHEAD – UPPER DEAN

The church is on the corner of a minor road, with Moat Farm on the other corner having a piece of topiary by the front door. Swineshead has a pleasant mixture of housing using all Bedfordshire's building materials. This road after a short distance becomes a grand track, very wide, lined with ash trees and enjoying a plentiful carpet of wild flowers. There are splendid high views in the east directly behind you, and the way ahead winds slowly up the contours.

Swineshead Wood, which lies across the nearby field, joins the route, and this dense, deciduous woodland contains a shrub-filled floor, whilst a high hedge on our other side creates a tunnel effect. A change of countryside again as the next stretch gives one the impression of a long narrow meadow filled with wild flowers, absolutely glorious; much in evidence are the silver-leaf and numerous grass types. It can be muddy in this region; also make sure you keep on the main route ignoring the track crossing, for hereabouts the tracks narrow and being closed in by high hedges and trees again there is a chance of going wrong. Five rows of poplar make something of a landmark alongside the young trees of Spanoak Wood, where we get a noticeable change of direction anti-clockwise.

Sandye Lane in front has the appearance of a green lane or drover's way, as indeed it may have been, bearing in mind that many of these countryside ways got adopted and when metalled became our country roads. Undulations in the fields are the only relief for this mile-and-a-half of near straight track, but those of a naturalist bent will observe the butterflies in season, especially the small browns and peacocks; besides, there's plenty of birdlife particularly of the game species. The north skyline is the Huntingdon District of Cambridgeshire, with the watershed on the northern slopes feeding the R. Til which flows through Tilbrook, which in turn becomes the R. Kym at Kimbolton, emptying into the R. Gt. Ouse at St. Neots.

Over a track crossing to descend onto the road when we go left and walk the entire length of Upper Dean High Street; stay on the right facing the oncoming traffic for you cannot be too careful. A straggling village of limestone cottages and a very well-proportioned stone church with a rather squat steeple. English bond brickwork of alternate header and stretcher bricks either in terracotta or the yellow Cambridgeshire brick seems the choice here.

On the abrupt tee junction marking the end of the High Street the road goes right, but we go left into a lane on a gentle gradient. Part way up, an overgrown lane is met on your right which has been deliberately left to allow its reversion to nature. However, alongside will be found a good track which follows the right hand hedgebanks; this turns left into a chestnut lined avenue, but we go on, using the grass headlands, passing an 'L' shaped brick, single-storey farmyard building. The winding grassy way passes wood pockets so make sure that you stay close to the sharp R.H. corner around Hay Wood. Look out for the path going into a remnant green lane as it is crossed diagonally by a just discernable path with nettles in patches. Leave by a broken pedestrian gate. Now make an alignment with Eastfields Farm, for this becomes a field crossing regardless of crops. However, it is possible to follow the perimeter track on the eastern side of the field as used by local horse riders. But before setting out for Eastfields Farm there is a chance to gain a view of Upper Dean windmill tower, seen in the distant hedgerows in the north, i.e. behind you.

Just before the farm we come across a pond, before fringing the farm by going left down the farm's drive road designated by a B.W., so arriving on a road tee junction. Go ahead on the Riseley road signposted slightly uphill, then on the first bend enter the L.H. field, for the B.W. is beside the hedge. This will now be on your R.H.S.; it might be a narrow path or just narrow headland. Actually, in taking this hedgerow walk, road walking is largely avoided and extra views are gained.

Unavoidably the road is regained finally, providing a tree-lined entry into Swineshead, though it could in fact be used all the way after leaving the Eastfields Farm Drive.

Bedfordshire Village Life

Places included: THURLEIGH – BLETSOE

Length of walk: 7 miles. The walk can be extended along the edge of the airfield, taking in Whitwickgreen round the pond and into Thurleigh Church End, making 9½ miles in all.

Grid Ref: Sheet 153 041 579.

Parking: Lay-by just off Old Milton Road start.

Bus services: 124.

Public Houses: The Jackal (Thurleigh).

Walk Links: Riseley road at northern limit of the walk links with Walk 4, and the road from Bletsoe into Sharnbrook leads out to Walk 1 for Harrold – Odell excursion.

Notes 1: Thurleigh airfield was considered along with Cublington (Wing, Bucks.) as a possible site for another London Airport in the 1970s.

2: Great views over the River Great Ouse valley are certainly a highlight of the walk, so don't choose a misty day and do take binoculars.

3: Thurleigh windmill tower along with Potton Tower make forlorn looking relics, a legacy from their heyday.

4: A remarkable collection of vintage farm waggons and equipment from a bygone day at Blackburn Hall comes as a surprise find for the walk.

BEDFORDSHIRE VILLAGE LIFE

A county gazetteer appeared recently, one of a series across England compiled from material sent by village Women's Institutes – 'The Bedfordshire Village Book'. Reading the book one is left with the impression that villages have undergone drastic change, but not total, for often as not the core and heart of the village remains, as one can observe for oneself. Expansion of the housing stock especially for commuters, fewer people working on the land directly or indirectly, fewer public houses, the village shops all but gone, even diminishing schools resulting in more bussing for the children. Interestingly villages in that book profile themselves under their origins pre- or post-Doomsday, also if they were known as lace-making or strawplait villages. The local great estates and their families in the 'big'

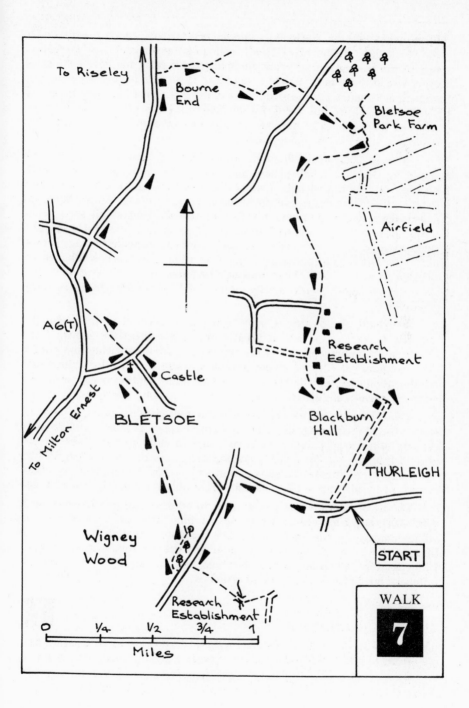

To Riseley

Bourne End

Bletsoe Park Farm

Airfield

A6(T)

To Milton Ernest

Castle

BLETSOE

Research Establishment

Blackburn Hall

THURLEIGH

START

Wigney Wood

Research Establishment

| 0 | ¼ | ½ | ¾ | 1 |

Miles

WALK

7

41

house get mentioned. Agriculture and horticulture played a major part over the years with 'Bedfordshire Gold', colloquial for Brussel sprouts, featuring, as did the pattern of roads thereabouts affecting the development or otherwise of the village. World Wars I and II seem to have made a greater impact on villagers than townsfolk for many experiences in those times are recounted. Taking out fields for airfields and the loss of the menfolk changed the fortunes of parishes. A war memorial or a memorial hall is entered in many of the monographs.

If asked what does village life centre around these days, my answer would be the village hall. These multi-functional buildings, usually with pleasing interiors, host talks, courses, games evenings (indoor bowls and badminton, for example), fund-raising and inter-village competitions, all good nights out. Continuing the list, there's dancing of all sorts, club meetings, produce shows and film shows, often on particular rural subjects such as canals or country railways. Compared with 'townies' village people have much more get-up-and-go in my estimation, and this is confirmed by the reports in the book. What must also be taken into consideration is that these people don't work locally and their commuting travel is often extensive.

Invariably the Institutes provide a potted account of their church, meaning C. of E., and are at great pains to document the growth from mostly unpretentious origins of the Baptist and Methodist churches within their boundaries. Clearly a considerable amount of inter-denominational collaboration goes on, whether on a rota basis or in joint services. Nowadays vicars or rectors are often looking after three or more churches.

Those keeping up the tradition of maypole dancing make a point of stating this in their village description – a most happy practice – and go on to list any other local peculiar customs, such as children with ears on the ground listening for the witches making their pancakes on Conger Hill in Toddington on Shrove Tuesday. Another regular topic concerns ghost claims, preferably more than one and preferably the non-frightening type.

The book contains many references to oddities and peculiarities, so I will let the reader have that pleasure of searching them out. Some of the past village characters and their habits are recounted, though the compilers thought it wise or discreet not to name the present folk who stand out. Unfortunately television induces levelling and conformity and under its influence one is less likely to be unorthodox.

WALK

7

THURLEIGH – BLETSOE

The walk starts from the lay-by signed Old Milton Road once being the way from Milton Ernest with the gaunt outline of Thurleigh Mill close by.

Because this particular road is not a right of way the first part of this walk must be on roads westwards initially away from Thurleigh. On reaching the crossroads turn to the left in the direction of Milton Ernest and in this section the roadside verges have controlled cutting programmes as they are nature reserves as on the Upper Staploe road. This provides some compensation for the road walking.

The giant complex of silo-like buildings being approached is in fact the R.A.E. Tunnel Site for test-work looking as if they belong to a power station. Enter the field at the southern end of Wigney Wood continuing round the back in a northward direction.

Go up to the old field gateway, entering a large field, and our direction is N.E. at about 30° to the L.H. hedgerow, making for the L.H.E. of the wood on the distant skyline. Do this regardless of the crops, if the path has not been re-instated, for Bletsoe is out of sight at this point. On reaching a cross-track, Bletsoe church tower comes into view and we gain marvellous vistas across the Gt. Ouse valley, west ranging round to the north – the highlight of the walk. Also, a series of lakes besides the river can be seen. Continue in this alignment until the corners of a pair of fields are met in a hedgerow. Now enter the top corner of the pasture, heading in the same direction to Bletsoe, making for the gate seen in the first of a series of fences. A slight change of direction follows aiming through the next fence gates towards the red roofs of the houses left of the church. We leave the fields by crossing a fence at the backs of the houses into Old Way, turning right on the road.

Several cast-iron water conduits with lions-head watersprouts stand along the roadside served as the community water supply. And this brings us up to Bletsoe church where a rest can be made, or we can wander the short distance beside the church to the site of Bletsoe castle and its St. John family and Tudor associations.

Opposite the churchyard one finds a telephone kiosk by a horse-breeding establishment specialising in Palamino horses here in Bletsoe. By the phone a concrete path having a F.P. sign leads out to a playing field beside a row of white bungalows of sheltered housing. On the far side one finds a rotten stile and bridge almost overgrown by bramble – take care and cut back the growth when crossing. There's a hedge on the L.H.S. of this arable field which takes the walk to the main road by the red house, and a stile part way along the fence gives access.

Continue forward, reaching Bourne End Road, which we use for our second bit of country road walking. Most people will look at 'The Roses', a thatched house beautifully set out on a crossroads with a propeller mounted on a thatched barn – must be of some significance. Quite wide views hereabouts are representative of this part of the county; in the course of time we come up to the Georgian well-proportioned Bourne End Farm in a warm terracotta brickwork relieved with consoled eaves.

Goodbye to the road, for behind the rear barns pass through an implement parking paddock into the arable fields again. Make sure you are going directly away from Bourne End Farm eastwards not the N.E. B.W. to Riseley, for our sights are on the Thurleigh Airfield. A word of caution, paths are to say the least indistinct in this part, for we go along a remnant hedgebank on its R.H.S., crossing into another field at the far end, veering a bit to the left if need be. Our general direction is for Park Farm and the tower by the wood at the end of the airfield, then when the road comes into view a dog-leg left around the last field will connect with a track leading to the road. Please note with the foregoing that the direction is as described, but you may find that neighbouring fields must be used dependent upon crops.

Finishing the walk presents no further problems. First cross the road and take the stone drive up the slope for Park Farm House (Bletsoe Farm on the map). On the far side of the farm go through the edge of the farm implement yard, bringing you up to the perimeter fence where not far away stands a tower-like building which one would assume to be a control tower from its form.

This fence now becomes our guide for the next few miles where the wide grass path provides access to every millimetre of the fence from the outside. Plenty of bramble hedges on your other side, and the path undulates as the end of the runway is rounded. In fact as far as plane spotters are concerned there does not seem much activity, just vast openness across the airfield. Towards the main entrance the course of the B.W. leaves the fence at a belt of bushes, utilising a track out to the entry road. Royal Aircraft Establishment, Bedford Airfield, Ministry of Defence, says the notice board as we press on back on a green field path by the fence, again taking a look at the hospital-like buildings and hangars on the runway side.

On turning the next corner stay with the fence going round the buildings, but we then go straight on using the track there ahead when the fence changes direction. And so down to Blackburn Hall Farm, a storage yard for masses of old farm equipment of a byegone age. Farm carts of all shapes and sizes, ploughs, elevators, harrows, binders, thrashing-drums, a gypsy caravan, mostly under cover, and there are tractors and lorries of varying vintage and on and on and on. Most of them are worthy of restoration – a veritable farm-museum waiting for a magic wand. The farm itself lies just about hidden, and we finish the walk down the farm drive onto the road after this peep into an 'Aladdin's cave'.

Bedfordshire Notables

> **Places included: BUSHMEAD – STAPLOE – COLMWORTH AREA**
>
> **Length of walk:** 5½ miles.
>
> **Grid Ref:** Sheet 153 127 599.
>
> **Parking:** Off road parking in the vicinity of the private road to Upper Honeydon Farm, but do not block field gateways.
>
> **Bus services:** 153.
>
> **Public Houses:** Colmworth.
>
> **Walk links:** None.
>
> **Notes 1:** Bushmead Priory can be seen only from the park.
>
> **2:** The Colmworth/Bolnhurst area does not lend itself for circular rambles being laced with country roads; they can be walked and are quite pleasant for that type of walking, but take a map for direction. (See further walking areas).

BEDFORDSHIRE NOTABLES

Whilst Bedfordshire might not rank with counties whose influence changed the course of the nation's history in a major way, the following list shows that the county had role-playing people. They might not have been born in the county in all instances but they had strong county connections nevertheless.

Albone, Daniel – Biggleswade
  Bicycle innovator and manufacturer.

Aragon, Catherine of
  The Queen of Henry VIII. Imprisoned in Ampthill Castle (now demolished). Divorce announced in Dunstable Priory.

Bunyan, John – born Harrowden, 1628 – Elstow/Bedford
  Evangelist, preacher and writer of "The Pilgrim's Progress", "Grace Abounding" and other works and tracts. Imprisoned in Bedford gaol. Truly Bedfordshire's son.

Dunstable, John (1380-1453) (John of Dunstable)
  Greatest of the early English composers. He perfected musical counterpoint.

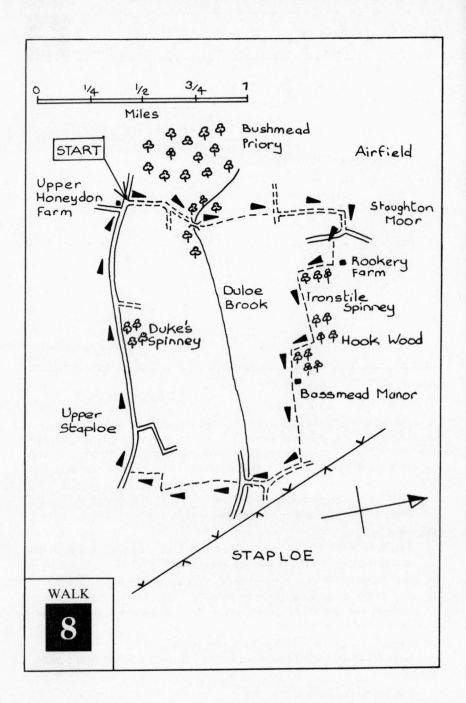

0   1/4   1/2   3/4   1
Miles

START

Bushmead Priory

Airfield

Upper Honeydon Farm

Stoughton Moor

Rookery Farm

Duloe Brook

Ironstile Spinney

Duke's Spinney

Hook Wood

Upper Staploe

Bossmead Manor

STAPLOE

WALK

8

Dunstable, Duke of
Fictitious Officer of the Guards in Gilbert and Sullivan's operetta 'Patience'.

de Greys of Wrest Park – Silsoe
Earls of the Realm. The 12th Earl made Duke of Kent.

Harpur, Sir William – Bedford. (born 1496)
London merchant-tailor, (Lord Mayor 1561). His bequest for Bedford School in 1566 enabled the foundation of the Harpur Trust, still administering four schools in the 1990s.

Howard, John (1726-1790) – Cardington
Investigator leading to the reform of prisons. Advocated the abolition of prisoners paying their gaolers for their food and bedding.

Howard, John – Bedford
Agricultural engineer. Plough improver and steam-ploughing and agricultural equipment manufacturer.

Loring, Sir Nigel – Chalgrave
Knight and indefatigable supporter and spokesman for Henry III. Naval battle of Sluys (1340), Battles of Crecy (1336) and Poitiers (1356).

Paxton, Sir Joseph – Milton Bryan
Gardener to the Dukes of Bedford and Devonshire (Chatsworth). Designer and constructor of the Crystal Palace, Hyde Park (1851) for the Great Exhibition.

Richardson, Sir Albert – Ampthill
Architect, restorer and conservation campaigner.

Russell family – Woburn Abbey
Dukes of Bedford.

Russell, John – Woburn Abbey
Whig politician and orator.

Smith, Worthington G. – Dunstable
Antiquarian, historian, botanist, identifier of horticultural diseases, fungi expert, architectural and botanical book illustrator.

Stannard family – Milton Bryan/Ampthill
Artists in water colours and oils.

Stewart, Sir Halley – Stewartby
Brickmaker extraordinary, (London Brick Co. consortium).

Tompion, Thomas (1639-1713) – Ickwell
Clockmaker extraordinary. London's finest long-case (grandfather) clockmaker.

Whitbread, Samuel – Southill
Brewing dynasty founder.

Wentworth, Henrietta – Toddington
Duke of Monmouth's love and saviour. Elopement.

This list cannot be considered definitive, only representative; then there's Falkes de Breauté and William de Beauchamp, both of Bedford; the Luke family of Cople and Lord and Lady Sundon – how do they feature prominently in Bedfordshire life? Their biographies, and a good few more, appear in 'Folk: characters and events in the history of Bedfordshire and Northamptonshire' by Vivienne Evans. An extensive index of people appears at the end of 'History of Bedfordshire' by Joyce Godber, whilst James Dyer's slim guide for 'Bedfordshire' contains some excellent biographies of many of those listed above and several notables not mentioned.

WALK

8

BUSHMEAD – STAPLOE – COLMWORTH AREA

Leave the road on a good gravel drive nearly opposite a pair of bungalows at the Upper Honeydon Farm road. Heading for the trees and proceed slightly right beside the tree-belt until a trackway crossing the fields is met. Continue forward till we come to an overgrown area, then enter diagonally right beside a small brick pump station. A good bridge takes us across the Duloe Brook and once over strike forward up the middle of a field that will almost certainly be planted with a crop.

Aim for the left end of the treeline on the brow. Three trees stand in a row in the field and by the middle one cross over a ditch. Then on reaching the big hedgerow go forward from the corner until a stone track from your left is met.

This makes a good position to look about, for across on the left through the trees stands the remaining building of Bushmeads Priory which could be visited when the walk is completed. In the low area by the Brook are the remnant fishponds of the Priory, now a lush overgrown area. The woodlands nearby acted as dispersal parking for aircraft in WWII for we are now not far away from the perimeter of Little Staughton airfield, the home of the Pathfinder Force of Bomber Command 1944-45 and the Squadrons of 8 Group.

There's a scattering of single storey buildings here for light industrial use, so the gate is crossed and we continue on the same line northwards on a good stone track on the R.H.S. of the trees till a gate bars the way. Open or get over the gate by the car-breaking yard and make your way round to your right.

On the tee junction bear right up to a Private No Access sign at a set of gates. Go through, then 50 yards on a hedge swings away from the road beside a concrete pad area. There are no signs in this quarter for walkers but don't be deterred for the rights of way are quite clearly shown on the O.S. Pathfinder map 980 (scale 1:25,000). Take care to stay on the correct rights of way.

Since the Duloe Brook you have been in the Huntingdon District of Cambridge and in a few moments will be crossing the county boundary again. In the next field on your left stands the buildings of Rookery Farm as you come up to a change of direction. Right at the end hedge onto a good stoney track which now follows this hedgerow, called Ironstile Spinney, to a gateway laced with barbed wire. However there is a bypass outlet through the spinney taking you out onto a track on the bend. Follow round left and into the next field and stop by the ditch going east to Hook Wood, the reason being that the right of way is on the north side which passes through to a wild lane beside that wood.

Turn south at the end along the outskirts of Home Wood on a good stone track to Bassmead Farm, and on meeting the farm sheds bear round in front of Bassmead Manor – a moated suite of timber-framed buildings – well worth a second look as you go by, then on by stone track out into the fields as if going to St. Neots. But we don't, for after about ½ mile we come to a tee junction of bridleways in front of two sets of grid lines. Go right here, for this is a clockwise walk, and right again where the tracks split down into Staploe. The stream here is the Duloe Brook, taking its name from the next village on its way to join the R. Gt. Ouse at Eaton Socon.

Cross the road, then beside the end row of houses our walk goes up the slope, following the L.H. hedge and out into the arable fields over the brow. When the boundary of a field is met that has the road on the far side, make a dog-leg to the right and follow the field edge down to the road.

Unfortunately the last leg entails a road walk, so this corner makes a suitable stopping point if wanted. But a word of warning; although traffic is light cars come through at quite a pace and since the road has many bends cars can appear unexpectedly.

So turn right in a westerly direction, first coming across Upper Staploe, a place of about three houses, and stay on the R.H.S. of the road. Keep on to reach Duke's Spinney – a wood of particular interest. The roadside verge only gets cut in the autumn because of the wild flowers, which are really an extension of the woodland growth. This pocket of mixed woodland has trees of varying heights and is designated as a Nature Reserve.

And so continue along the road back to the walk's commencement.

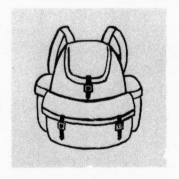

Bedfordshire's Rivers

Places included: GREAT BARFORD – TEMPSFORD – BLUNHAM – OUTSKIRTS OF BEDFORD

Length of walk: 1. 11 miles starting from the Renhold turn-off on A428(T).
2. 5¼ miles, same start, along river to Gt. Barford and back same way.
3. 5¾ miles, starting from Gt. Barford to Tempsford and Blunham circular to Gt. Barford.

Grid Ref: Sheet 153 108 514.

Parking: Use the layby at the top of Hill Farm road, and before starting off look for the motte and bailey earthwork behind the hedge.

Bus services: X1, X3, X4, 112 and 152 (U.C.).

Public Houses: The Anchor Inn and The Beehive (Gt. Barford) and The Wheatsheaf (Tempsford).

Walk Links: Willington Lock to Willington riverside walk on old railway bed for Walk 10.

Notes 1: Quite an arduous walk, especially on the northern riverside section. Take a stick to beat down undergrowth by the river covering the path.

  2: The Gt. Ouse has not got the character and attractions of the stretch to the west of Bedford, but for the Bedfordshire walker this walk is a must.

  3: Roxton Park to the north of Tempsford has major traction engine rallies.

BEDFORDSHIRE'S RIVERS

Bedfordshire's principal river, the River Gt. Ouse, rises in the Banbury/ Bicester area, taking a 150-mile course out into The Wash at Kings Lynn. The name Ouse is considered Celtic in origin, probably meaning 'water with a leisurely flow'. On its banks stand pollarded willows – this is virtually coppicing at eight feet above the ground, keeping the crop of branches out of the way of grazing animals. Oak, beech and ash can also be pollarded. East Anglia has a Little Ouse River originating south of Thetford, whilst York stands on a River Ouse, hence the need for differentiation.

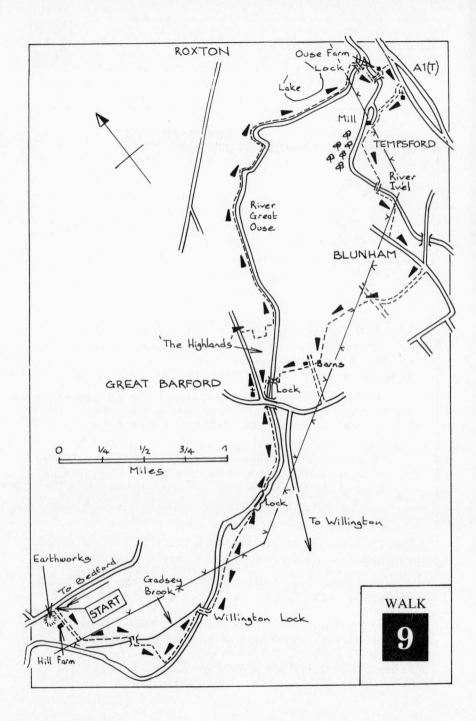

ROXTON

Ouse Farm
Lock

Lake

A1(T)

Mill

TEMPSFORD

River
Ivel

River
Great
Ouse

BLUNHAM

'The Highlands

Barns

GREAT BARFORD

Lock

Lock

To Willington

Earthworks

To Bedford

Gadsey
Brook

START

Willington Lock

Hill Farm

O   1/4   1/2   3/4   1
Miles

WALK

9

52

The River Gt. Ouse is joined by the River Ivel at Tempsford, flowing north through St. Neots, Huntingdon and Ely. Its course in the county is littered with stretches of water marking spent gravel workings. Whilst on the subject of the Gt. Ouse, the rivers Til (Tilbrook) and Kym on the county boundary (Kimbolton) gain waters from north Bedfordshire before flowing into the Gt. Ouse. Actually both places are in Northamptonshire.

Going in a clockwise direction we find the River Ivel in Biggleswade out of Baldock, taking the waters of the River Flit rising in the Flitwick/Flitton area and the River Hiz from Hitchin. Cambridge's beloved River Cam has its headwaters in the springs at Ashwell, Herts, forming the county boundary as the River Rhee just south of Wrestlingworth.

In the south of the county is the River Lea starting life in Leagrave Marsh, Luton, flowing into the River Thames in Dockland, having journeyed through Hertford, Ware and Enfield.

St. Albans' River Ver has the dip slopes of Dunstable Downs as its catchment area and is a tributary of the River Colne, going out through Watford before emptying into the River Thames near Slough.

On the western side flows the River Ouzel alongside the canal at Leighton Buzzard, then finding its way into the River Gt. Ouse at Newport Pagnell. The Ouzel springs from just north of Dunstable with the confluence of the Clipstone Brook from the Milton Bryan/Toddington watersheds and brooks in the Vale of Aylesbury.

Some of the surface waters in the north-west region of Bedfordshire enter the River Nene at Rushden (flowing from Northampton), onwards to Peterborough before swelling the River Welland at Spalding, thence out into The Wash.

WALK

GREAT BARFORD – TEMPSFORD – BLUNHAM – OUTSKIRTS OF BEDFORD

9

Walk down Hill Farm road which terminates at a gateway leading into water meadows; the parking here is reserved for anglers. The walk proper then starts.

Cross a stile by the gate and turn sharp left under the grid system, whilst across the meadow flows the Gt. Ouse, seen a great deal on this walk. This long narrow field contains willows beside a depression that may or may not have water; it is recorded on maps as Gadsey Brook. (Sections elsewhere do have water, since the area takes field drainage from the northern slopes). A bridge crosses the brook right at the end, then it makes a left turn into a short lane connecting two fields; when out of the link take a direct route against the fence to the river. This is not the true course but more convenient, since it all depends on the agriculture here.

Now along the river bank on an embankment punctuated by anglers' pitch pegs, cross the stile and stay by the river's edge – makes one think of

53

"Wind in the Willows" or "Three Men in a Boat". The path takes some finding, being rather indistinct in the long grass, before rejoining another section of the anglers' path. Next feature we meet takes the form of Willington Lock and Weir – all very modern and functional. In crossing the river by the footbridge one realises that the river does not flow freely but is really a series of spillway dams just like the R. Thames. On the other bank, all neatly mown grass, leaves the link for the Willington/Cople walk, but we go north having six fields of varying sizes to go through beside the river. Notice how gravelly the soils are in the fields; no wonder the Gt. Ouse valley has had extensive surface mineral extraction – several of the sites are now flooded as nature reserves.

A footbridge over a disused brick-sided lock takes us into a confined area, where a path on the left side of what might be presumed to be a lock-keeper's cottage hugs the water's edge under the trees. An arched wooden bridge gives a crossing for the main watercourse in an area used for boat moorings.

Back on the north bank we find a rough path, if it can be called such, then follow four fields for negotiation, with enjoyable riverine scenery. The last field before reaching Gt. Barford contains Jacob's sheep, but the greater interest must be the bridge itself. Alterations are readily apparent and you might find the dentilated arches an unusual characteristic. The bridge has ten arches with six more in the abutments. 'The Bedfordshire Magazine' has had several accounts of Bedfordshire bridges (R. Ivel included) giving a history of origin, alteration, floods and mishaps across the centuries. In addition to this quarterly magazine one can find documentary information in the excellent County Record Office.

A word of warning concerning the next section into Tempsford, for it's best to have a stick to clear the way in places, but do not be deterred, for the more who walk this stretch the better the condition. Besides, there are scenic rewards.

Traffic lights here regulate single line traffic for the bridge, and we go on the road out of Gt. Barford by Bridge Cottage with the church on the other side and the Anchor Inn P.H., leaving behind the riverside lawns where we will make our return. A Scout camp site gets followed by the forlorn-looking 'The Highlands' residence, but keep going until the sewerage works have been passed. Straightway turn into the field, traversing round behind the works before making directly for the river.

From now on one stays tight by the river, in places pushing through burdock, thistle and nettles on the narrow confines between fences and the water's edge. Conditions are variable, even decent in places kept open by anglers; also be careful at footbridges, for they are not all in good condition, even where brooks flow into the river. A good many stiles must be crossed, so it's pointless noting every obstacle – just keep going. You will find the direction gradually changes from northwards round to eastwards.

Eventually a man-made lake comes into view, screened by Leylandii cypresses, concluding this part with a footbridge over the Gt. Ouse at Roxton Weir, Tempsford.

Before moving on take a look at the confluence of the R. Ivel with the Gt. Ouse – a reward for all that effort and it's altogether easier from now onwards, honestly! Take to the banks of the Ivel, which being shallow, lets you see the gravelly bed and the drifting water-weed in the currents – the wooded overhanging banks make good cover for water loving birds, especially around the sill in the water. A bridge into Ouse Farm leads to a brick-stepped stile, then through the concreted yard and out left, making sure the yard gate is closed. Then up the farm road into Tempsford. Tempsford has a quiet air, since the A1 traffic pours by on the bypass. Go right to the church with its striking stone-block churchyard wall and lych-gate. Possibly you might like to take a look at the village before moving on, and The Wheatsheaf P.H. can waylay you. Beside the church leaves Mill Lane for the return route, where Church Barn has been converted into a house. The sight before us is commanded by three sluices on the right of Mill House, behind which the river is channelled into a mill pond. Hereabouts stood Gannocks castle of Danish origin, nothing now to be seen, whilst we continue on this excellent trackway beside a spillway backwater and the rural mill gardens leading us up to a gate and a stile.

Sharp left after the stile in a grazing field in the east can be seen the A1(T) and, beyond, the railway embankment of the Kings Cross to York line. Shortly a field bridge must be crossed, then comes a high hand-railed footbridge over the Ivel and we continue southerly on the western bank. The river here flows through open fields in yet another riparian variant, having a width of twenty feet or more confined by high banks; we go under grid lines. Then, just before going into a stretch of woodland, turn away from the river (the last time we shall see the R. Ivel) through the edge of a market-gardening field and go parallel with the grid, thence out onto the road by the Anglian Water control station. Left down this minor road in the direction of Blunham to the point where Grange Road meets the main road. If you wish to take a saunter into Blunham now is your chance, for it's here that we change direction on a gravel drive between high hedges at the F.P. sign. In the fields given over to market gardening the scattering of greenhouses confirms the staple industry, and glimpses of the four-pinnacled high church tower lend a focal point for Blunham. The track bears to the right at the end in a northward direction and it is here we stop and take stock of the next section.

Nearly ¾ mile of crop walking lies ahead to Gt. Barford since all other alternatives are not rights of way, so don't be frightened if you are the first to rewalk the field, for as yet there are no F/P signs for guidance. Refer to the sketch map for direction.

Keeping in the same direction you have just walked look across to see Gt. Barford church in the distance and commence making for just to the right of the church tower. There may be more than one crop in this giant field and for the first bit aim for the R.H.S. of the pylon in front, then when you have walked the same distance again make a 30° turn to the left away from the church tower. The next change of direction comes when you are in line with the track alongside a row of trees besides three barns. This takes us to the river, having crossed over a field track by the barns. The sketch map and O.S. maps makes this clear.

Gt. Barford is in full view from here, stretching back away from the river, so after the trackway bridge go right beside the stream and the line of limes. The path, though not clear, can be discerned entering the riverside recreation area by a caravan camping site. Make your way to the river, then cross, using the footbridge spanning the lock and weir, making use of the path by the moorings' lawns up to Gt. Barford bridge.

Dependent upon how you planned your walk the next decision rests with you. Maybe a car awaits you, or like me you could make the return to Hill Farm starting near the Renhold turn-off on the A428(T) outside Goldington, or alternatively you could end up in Willington or Cople. By the way, if walking back to the original start take care when seeking the arched footbridge back to the derelict lock, for you can easily overshoot on the river's edge and find out you have to cover some distance retracing your steps.

Bedfordshire Airships I – The Cardington Airship Sheds

Places included: WILLINGTON – COPLE

Length of walk: 5 miles.

Grid Ref: Sheet 153 106 500.

Parking: Park conveniently off the road near the National Trust Dovecote and Stables, Willington.

Bus services: 176, 177 and 178.

Public Houses: The Crown (Willington) and Five Bells (Cople).

Walk links 1: Willington village to Willington lock joins up with Walk 9.

2: Priory Country Park can be visited from the A5134 Bedford to Sandy road.

3: A link can be made with Elstow by walking through Cardington and Harrowden from Cople for Walk 16.

4: Access with Walk 11 can be made from Water End south of Cople by bridleway near cutting and tunnel through to Warden Street, or by path from Wood End Farm out to Sweetbriar Farm on the Greensand Ridge Walk.

Notes 1: Harrowden was the birthplace of John Bunyan in 1628 and with so many books on the man I am not contributing a thumbnail sketch of Bedfordshire's greatest notable. Cardington should be mentioned as having connections with the Howard and Whitbread families.

2: Shortstown close by Harrowden and Cardington is named after Short Bros., the aviation constructors.

3: This walk and Walk 16 offer good views of the airship sheds with a close-up gained from the A600 road.

BEDFORDSHIRE'S AIRSHIPS I – THE CARDINGTON AIRSHIP SHEDS

Between August 1916 and April 1917 A. J. Main and Co. of Glasgow built the first airship hangar shed at Cardington measuring 700 ft. by 254 ft. with an overall height of 145 ft. The heavily ballasted self-supporting double doors moved sideways on multiple flanged wheel bogies, which took half an hour's work on four capstans for a team of labourers to fully open.

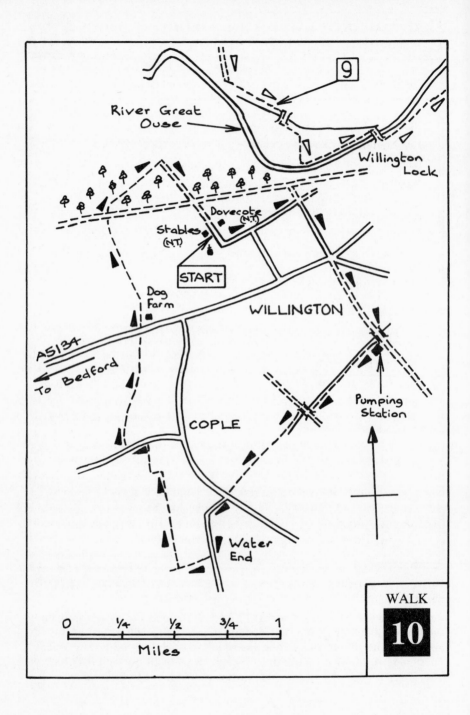

9

River Great
Ouse

Willington
Lock

Dovecote
(N.T.)

Stables
(N.T.)

START

Dog
Farm

WILLINGTON

A5134

To Bedford

COPLE

Pumping
Station

Water
End

0   ¼   ½   ¾   1

Miles

WALK

10

The decision in 1924 for the construction of the R100 at Howden, Yorks and the R101 at Cardington, by then known as the Air Ministry's Royal Airship Works, meant shed enlargements. On completion in May 1927 at a cost of £105,000 by the Darlington based Cleveland Bridge and Engineering Co. the new dimensions became 812 ft. (248 m.) long by 272 ft. (84 m.) wide and 186 ft. (55 m.) at its apex. This was possible because of its bolted construction, necessitating dismantling whilst the 'A' frame girders were modified on site, before re-erection on correspondingly stronger footings. A seven-ton crane and 140 ft. jib working on the site built a 230 ton stage, 100 ft. wide, 80 ft. long and 120 ft. high, moved on tracks wire-hauled by winches carrying two ten-ton steam cranes each with 110 ft jibs. Using this equipment the original doors and shed were dismantled, altered in Darlington, then re-erected. The new doors, being 46 ft. higher, required an increased base width for their tracks and can carry between 33 and 60 tons per wheel, dependent upon the prevailing wind strength. These doors each weigh 470 tons and after modification are now electrically powered.

The area inside the shed measures 4¾ acres (2 hectares), serviced by three internal gangways the length of the roof and high level transverse corridors reached by three staircases on both sides of the shed.

Pulham in Norfolk had another comparable airship shed, scene of the R33 trials; in 1924 this particular hangar was transported, slightly enlarged, and re-erected as the No. 2 hangar in Cardington, meeting the same sizes as its neighbour. In all the operation cost an estimated £100,000, again carried out by the Cleveland Bridge and Engineering Co. Each shed contains something like 4,000 tons of steel.

Disaster struck in October 1930 when the hydrogen-filled R101 crashed at Beauvais, France, with a loss of 48 lives by fire, as did the German 'Hindenberg' in 1937 at Lakehurst, New York – both rigid airships being the subject of a number of accounts and books. Although the R100 private venture had an unblemished record, with the termination of airship development the R100 raised £450 when broken up and sold as scrap.

Cardington continued as a base for balloon development, taking the official title of Balloon Development Establishment in 1938, having already been the R.A.F. training base for balloon operators for two years. Balloons tethered by winches over London in the last war and the accompanying searchlights and anti-aircraft guns will be a sight still remembered by a good few people. Cardington saw service as a calling-up centre for those doing their National Service in the R.A.F. in the post-war years.

On signposts and maps the name Shortstown appears close to Cardington. Short Brothers were responsible for the airship constructions here and may be better known as the Isle of Wight aircraft company, builder of the famous Sunderland flying boat which did such sterling work in the last war.

WILLINGTON – COPLE

Set off on the road you probably drove in on, only this time spare a second look for the striking St. Lawrence church, a notable building in the form of a double nave, showing distinct periods of architecture. Round the corner and keep walking past the school and on to the corner where the Methodist church stands. On the left a concrete road on the other side of a wooden gate provides a connection with the river and thence on the old railway bed to Willington lock and the Gt. Barford/Tempsford walk link. Actually, the railway bed gets used later in the walk and the real link joins up with the Willington start; it should be mentioned we don't see the R. Gt. Ouse on this walk but see conclusion. Down the road, passing the Crown P.H., to 'The Timbers', an AD1622 timber-framed house, complete with brick noggin and leaded windows; there's another gem on the opposite corner of this junction. We leave the houses of Willington by going down Wood Lane across the main road. The sign states 'No through road', with the road surface changing into stone as we leave the last of the houses. Unfortunately an unattractive car rubbish dump mars the area, but we go out into the fields toward the distant Sheerhatch wood on the hillside as we go in the direction of the lonely Hill Farm.

A bridge about ¾ mile out of the village indicates a change of direction when a gas control compound comes into sight and we go right through a gate for a track between the compound and the deep water-filled ditch. In the course of time a cross track is met in front of a farm implement shed, so change ditch banks via the bridge, walking this time on the Cople side of the water, proceeding in the direction of the airship hangars. The headland looks doubtful, for there may not be a path; only odd trees and marginal hedges dot the landscape nearby, and on this stretch we find the ends of a couple of tracks coming out of the Cople area. This in turn finishes beside a quite remarkable Rose cottage, with some clever architectural designed extensions in the form of a comparable building linked by a single-storey link, both given a pebble-dash finish harmonising the old and the new.

At Water End set out ahead from this tee road junction, taking us, on rounding the bend, into a cluster of houses of differing styles, materials and ages. Country gardens complete the picture in this eye-catching spot. On reaching the last house on your right a B.W. commences in a short green lane entering quite a long field.

Just more than halfway along this field end a gap gains access to some old sheds. The direction becomes northwards on a good track, gaining us vantage for the rear side of the Water End cottages – the back of a house can inform a lot about the construction of a building. Cardington's airship sheds demand attention, with the chance of catching sight of one of Airship

Industries' products, an interesting prospect. This long straight B.W. brings the walker to the edge of a sports field, skirted left before coming out on the Cople/Cardington road. Go left here beside a stream feeding a small pond, stopping when you reach the road bridge culvert.

On the other side a B.W. sets off against a water-filled ditch. The map shows the whole of the next section as disused workings, so don't be surprised at the nettles and low branches, as nature re-asserts herself. Very wild, as willows colonise the grasslands along with a seemingly endless multitude of different shrubs in a wetland habitat. As far as walking goes, the path presents no problems. In the right season dragon-flies and damsel-flies hover about the area, confirming the nature of the ground. In fact, numbers of man-made ponds abound in the area around Cople, from the extraction days. It should be observed that the R. Gt. Ouse and Bedford's Priory Park are not that far away.

And we meet the main road opposite the Dog Farm start of our next leg. A good track leads from their yard through linked small fields, and bullrushes grow by the overgrown stretches of water. The trees and hedges all around the riverside area give an arboreal atmosphere. Then we come upon the perimeter tree belt surrounding mineral workings; here the green lane is in fact the bed of the Bedford/Sandy railway line. This green way can be used to go almost direct to the start and on to Willington lock if you so wish. It seems that the whole area of this wooded bend in the river gets walked by many people. Little wonder, it's so refreshing – a lung close by a big town. But we go into the shelter belt, turning right, using the green arrows as guides in this woodland trail. Lots of extra tree planting has been going on, reinforcing this screen belt.

You will have noticed that progressively we have been diverging away from the perimeter tree belt. Now we come upon a crossing of ways and take the right direction; this becomes the last stretch to finish the excursion. Passing across the screen belt the track becomes a road near a bowls club, and the road enters open lands on both sides as we re-approach the Willington Dovecote and Stables (the only National Trust buildings in Bedfordshire).

Bedfordshire's Agricultural Colleges

Places included: OLD WARDEN – WARDEN STREET

Length of walk: 4 miles. Instead of taking the field walk to the church for the conclusion, photographers may like to walk all of Old Warden.

Grid Ref: Sheet 153 137 444.

Parking: Church car park. Donations requested in the box provided, for church restoration work.

Bus services: 180.

Public Houses: Hare and Hounds (Old Warden).

Walk Links 1: For Walk 15 use the roads through Warden Warren and Southill from Old Warden.

2: The Greensand Ridge Walk passes through Sweetbriar Farm on the northwest side of this walk.

Notes 1: Old Warden church, built in sandstone, has many fine details from earlier ecclestiastical ages, which inlude a double-decker pew close by the door. An abundance of stained glass lights the church and the floor has encaustic tiles, whilst the wealth of carvings bear angels and masks in low relief – even the door has crockets on the ribs. Please make a donation to one of Bedfordshire's most distinctive churches.

2: The Shuttleworth Vintage Aircraft Museum, just outside Old Warden, can be counted a Bedfordshire 'must' and their regular flying displays are advertised in the county press. Next door on the same road one finds the recently restored Swiss Garden in the care of Bedfordshire C.C., with adjacent car parking.

3: The Tudor remnant of Warden Abbey can be seen from Warden Street – now a farm once in the Gostwicks' ownership stands on the site of a Cistertian 1135 foundation. The monks cultivated the once well-known Warden cooking pear.

BEDFORDSHIRE'S AGRICULTURAL COLLEGES

Should the subject of agricultural 'seats of learning and research' arise one can say that Bedfordshire makes a more than average contribution as the prospectuses of various universities and colleges of further education will

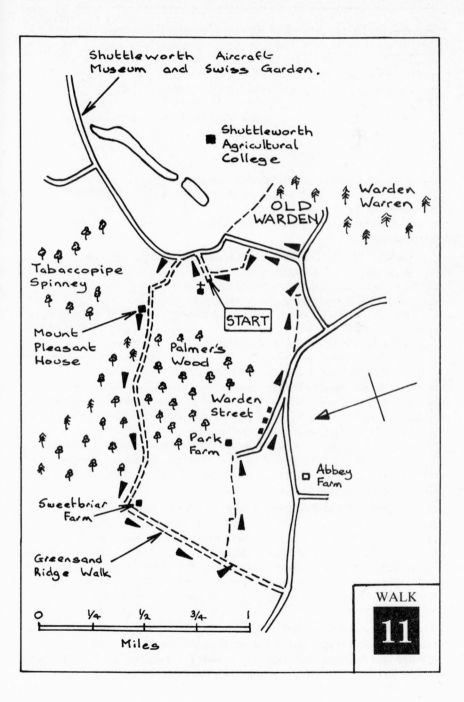

Shuttleworth Aircraft
Museum and Swiss Garden.

Shuttleworth
Agricultural
College

Warden
Warren

OLD
WARDEN

Tabaccopipe
Spinney

START

Mount
Pleasant
House

Palmer's
Wood

Warden
Street

Park
Farm

Abbey
Farm

Sweetbriar
Farm

Greensand
Ridge Walk

0   ¼   ½   ¾   1
Miles

WALK

11

indicate. **Premier in the field of agricultural education in the county must be the Cranfield Institute of Technology, offering degree courses in Agricultural Engineering and Rural Resource Management at the Silsoe College. Courses in forage, feed cereal and vegetable crops, sheep and pig production and, as may be expected, courses concerned with tractors, power-units and mechanisation. It might be worth mentioning that the Cranfield Institute of Technology at Cranfield airfield, seen on that particular walk, provides M.Sc. courses in such advanced subjects as Thermal Process Engineering, Industrial Robotics, Machine and Product Design and Advanced Manufacturing Technology.**

Back to agriculture, Old Warden's Shuttleworth College's contribution lies in the provision of advanced courses in animal husbandry, farm management and several other aspects of agriculture. Overseas students attend their courses and the college possesses a noted library on kindred subjects.

Possibly the best known establishment, but this time for research, would be what was the National Institute of Agricultural Engineering, also at Silsoe, in the ancestral home of the de Greys in Wrest Park. Known these days at AFRC Engineering (an Agricultural and Food Research Council institute, one of twelve) their spheres of activity come as something of an eye-opener since they list:- strategic research; process and rural environment control for the health of farmworkers and animal welfare; investigation into tractor and self-propelled machines; materials for implements; cultivation; crop establishment and protection; harvesting; processing, storage and handling of forage, then we can add their work in arable and greenhouse crops' cultivation. Building design comes in for consideration as do farms, livestock houses, green- and mushroom-houses then lastly milking 'parlours'. (Strange term really, for parlour and parliament both mean places where you go and talk, from the French verb parler = to speak. I digress.) Mention must be made of their Overseas Division, taking agricultural engineering skills into the developing countries. And still the list of their involvements could go on.

Unilever's Food Research Centre primarily involved in human foods, animal nutrition and the biological testing of all Unilever's products has as its centre Colworth House, Sharnbrook. The modern laboratories undertake work for Birds Eye Foods and include such brand names as Walls, Mattesson, Batchelors, Lipton, and several European continental manufacturers, especially fish products for Unilever with an Anglo-Dutch parentage. Well over 1,000 people work at this, the largest food research laboratory in Western Europe.

All aspects of fish processing from catching through to the disposing of the waste as fishmeal or any other product, but particularly aspects of fish-freezing come in for investigation. Canned vegetables; meat, dairy and dessert products; dehydrated complete meals, cooking oils and of course

margarine appear in their coverage. Analysts and bacteriologists work on the collective knowledge of biological systems in food products.

Husborne Crawley enters this subject in having an out-station of the Rothamsted Experimental Station, Harpenden, Herts. For here in Bedfordshire they can make comparative crop studies on the lighter sandy soils of the Greensand against the heavier soils on their Hertfordshire lands.

Botany is taught in most schools together, in varying degrees of depth, with the related subjects of geography, geology and topography, which all have a direct bearing on the social sciences. A look at the prospectuses of the county's colleges of further education shows that these subjects are also not neglected there.

WALK

OLD WARDEN – WARDEN STREET

Having made a donation towards church funds in the collection box for parking, go down the holly-lined lane you just drove up, meeting the through road near an eyebrow-thatched cottage. This is the road for the Shuttleworth Air Museum and the locally equally famous Swiss Garden; head in that direction, passing a hand pump in a rustic shelter. Where the road bends, take the L.H. bridleway marked Mount Pleasant; it is a made-up tree-lined road. On the neighbouring hill stands the Old Warden church, and before us we look out over the long lake in the Shuttleworth estates – the family home is now an Agricultural College and cannot be visited – whilst on the horizon is the Sandy T.V. mast, set against the sky. Curve left through the Mount Pleasant farmyard, then after a pair of cottages the trackway becomes stoney, and there are the tell-tale signs of pheasant rearing in the nearby trees. Ahead is a broad avenue in the light airy woodland of Palmer's Wood, then on leaving the woodland a row of oaks in a hedgerow is followed – I hope they remain – now proceeding across fields to the side of Sweetbriar Farm. Pockets of woodland show up in the countryside in all directions.

The paths or tracks are not at all distinct here and one has gone completely missing, so continue past the farm until the end of a woodbelt coming up from your right is met from the N.E. and a bridleway is found. And once again we meet the G.R.W. on its way in the direction of Northill, Sandy and Gamlingay (Cambs.), the termination. Now we know where we are, turn left at the field edges along a line of trees beside a well defined bridleway used as the G.R.W., signed with marker posts.

Bedford and its environs stretch out in the distance on the north side of this ridge, and we stay on the Way for a little while. Ignore the footpath crossing marked by green arrows but stop at the major bridleway junction. Across the field ahead is a wooded bank which is the spoil of the cutting for the dismantled Bedford/Shefford/Elstow railway line. Now turn left toward the R.H.E. of Palmer's Wood on a bridleway well used by tractors, and a pair of white posts and rails denote the whereabouts of pipeline beside a R. H. ditch. After about ¾ mile, losing height all the time, a derelict dutch barn is observed and the way becomes a path between two overgrown hedges. This stretch is kept open by riders and therefore has the distinct possibility of being muddy.

Stay on this winding track, which skirts Park Farm complete with its duck pond, but when you turn the final corner take a look at the interesting composition of the farm building and its end wings. The centre entry projection makes an 'E' for its plan. Now onto the road surface of Warden Street, getting a good sighting of Abbey Farm south on your right. A tall Tudor chimney on a gabled short building has a round tower at the rear – read the history of Warden Abbey for yourself if it whets your appetite.

The Street now onward has trim mown grass verges, but the feature are the Samuel Whitbread 1775 diamond-paned cottages bearing plates commemorating their renovation during 1860. Join the Cardington to Old Warden road by turning left, then leave this on the first bend just past a farm access road at the F.P. sign and turn almost immediately into the next field R. through a gap in the hedgerow. Follow the next hedgerow until a gap is reached close by the houses. Now turn R. under the power cables and follow the garden boundary back to the road and then turn left. This has reduced the amount of roadwalking.

Down the road, making for Old Warden road junction, but keep an eye open for the made-up footpath just inside the field boundary close by the Anglian Water Authority sub-station. This avoids roadwalking, at the same time catching sight of the unique cottages, one of which has a pulley-wheel on a well-head. The road is regained shortly, passing the village school.

Old Warden retains its village shop, housed in the old stables, distinguished by a ventilator tower on the roof and a large black and gilt clock set in the roadside end wall. Close by is the Hare and Hounds P.H. Opposite the shop is a path out into the fields between two trimmed hedges with even a seat at the entrance. Wooden steps up an embankment next, then stay right at the garden end of a large residence, before going R. through a kissing gate. Cross the donkey field towards the church and a second chance of the rather fine distant view.

Food for Thought

Places included: BIGGLESWADE – BROOM

Length of walk: 6½ miles.

Grid Ref: Sheet 153 187 444.

Parking: Park in the side roads on the western side of Mill Lane in Biggleswade (off A6001).

Bus services: 176, 177 and 180.

Public Houses: White Horse and The Cock (Broom) and pubs in Biggleswade.

Walk Links 1: Road link on western extremity of walk through Warden Warren into Old Warden.

2: Using the B1040 road out of Biggleswade for Potton joins Walk 13.

3: Roads from Broom to Stanford or via Southill reach Walk 15.

Notes 1: An extension can be made using bridleways behind the Old Warden airfield to see Ickwell's famous high maypole.

FOOD FOR THOUGHT

Holme Mills, just south of Biggleswade and valued at 47 shillings in the 1086 Domesday Book, may not be instantly recognised, hiding behind a mature tree screen, but all shoppers will in fact know the logo of the Jordan family, cereal millers since 1855. Sacks of corn lifted by a sack hoist housed in a gable appear in the centre of the logo vignette. The flour mill is still powered by a Gilbert and Gilkes water turbine installed in 1896. Gas engines superseded the water-wheel as happened in many wind-powered corn mills and they in turn gave way to electric drives. A visit to Bromham water-mill gives one a good idea of the layout of water-powered milling.

Jordan's shop at the mill is an epicure's delight, set out with 'old fashioned' shopkeeper's shelving, while sacks of their products in front of the counter are reminiscent of the corn merchant establishments. There are conserves and honey, along with a host of oat products bearing the 'Original Crunchy' label, cereals with fruit, cereal bars of all flavours and of course the ubiquitous muesli, for they are in the business of whole foods – more later.

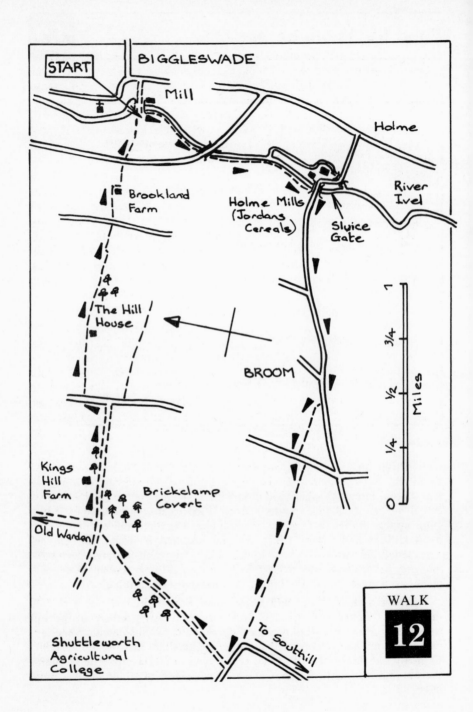

BIGGLESWADE

START

Mill

Holme

Brookland Farm

Holme Mills (Jordans Cereals)

River Ivel

Sluice Gate

The Hill House

BROOM

1

3/4

Miles

1/2

1/4

0

Kings Hill Farm

Brickclamp Covert

Old Warden

To Southill

Shuttleworth Agricultural College

WALK

12

The company's turnover in 1988 of £10 million for 5,000 tonnes of oat-based foods reflects a customer demand for healthy food, and the demand goes on increasing. So what lies behind this phenomenon? Elsewhere in this book one reads of farming practices in Bedfordshire and the concentration of agricultural learning in the county with the possible demise of agricultural research as part of government policy – see 'Sword of Damocles'. Jordan's health food philosophy makes its own special Bedfordshire agricultural contribution. This becomes even more pertinent now that the supermarkets have discovered a 'green' vocabulary in response to customer pressures.

Jordans were one of the founder members of the Guild of Conservation Food Products and the Organic Food Manufacturers Federation, with over 240 farmers contracted with them for the harvest of Conservation and Organic Grade cereals. Conservation Grades forbid more than 200 conventional agrochemicals which leave toxic residues in the crop and soil, whereas Organic Grades prevent the use of any artificial fertilisers, herbicides or pesticides whatsoever. In the latter grade a two-year conversion period must be met, eliminating present soil residues and meeting standards controlled by the Soil Association. Both grades are assessed by independent inspectors.

1970 saw the launch of the Jordan whole food cereals, with claims for high fibre and of being a 100% product with no additives. Then in the period 1975 to 1985 consumers became increasingly aware of health foods and wanted to know what 'E' numbers were all about. Come 1988, environmental issues reflected public concern for planet Earth and its atmosphere, and 'Green' reports and guides came to the fore, (see Further Reading). At the same time fears about fats, sugars and salt in food products caused considerable concern, along with the various functions of 'E' number additives now listed on food packaging.

But all this must be set against the wider context of the world environment, and walkers being country lovers cannot ignore the issues. Be it chemical additives in food, supermarkets developing green field sites, loss of forests in the world for pulping, land hunger, wastes of every conceivable description discharged into the atmosphere, rivers and seas, there is no escape. Inhabitants of the world are both victims and participants, for what is at issue is destruction left for future generations to sort out, caused by cash starvation and lack of will power on the part of various of the world's governments.

As with all 'movements' concerned with politically sensitive issues the 'greening' has come from those concerned, as supermarkets have admitted they would not willingly have put environmentally friendly products on their shelves, but they quickly saw the importance of public awareness and opinion. All a very deep, involved subject but it is well worth reading the articles in the responsible press and the now very readable books on these issues.

Look for the Soil Association and Organic Farmers and Growers logos on food products, showing crops were grown on chemically free soils and the livestock not reared under intensive conditions. Bedfordshire's Jordans set the pace and still continue their research, being committed to the consumption of purer foods.

BIGGLESWADE – BROOM

Mill Lane is the start and finish of this walk, wherever you have left your car. The three-storey mill here has been converted into flats, keeping the integrity of the mill as a whole, but look out for the mill-stones set into the cobbles surrounding the mill – a very nice touch. This provides a unique opportunity to see the millwright's 'harp' cuts in these stones. These assist the movement of the grain when milled between the fixed 'bed' stone and the 'runner''. Across from the mill the field serves as a play area with access to the water's edge – a happy haunt for children.

On our way now, firstly crossing the fast flowing waters in the weir, then turning left onto the asphalt path beside the river, with a recreation ground on your other hand. In a short time this becomes a grassy stretch, before entering a riverside path when a footbridge over a side stream has been crossed. The River Ivel has a width of about 25' here. The next stretch has overgrown river banks and quite a bit of anglers' rubbish, but takes us right up to the A1 Biggleswade by-pass, carried on a concrete flyover of proportions reminding one of Westminster bridge. The banks have been cleared of undergrowth but deposits of rubbish remain, and one realises that the river is not really very fast flowing, all because of the back-up effect of the weir. Leaving the noisy A1 behind, the river narrows to approximately 20', and a pleasant riverine atmosphere prevails, with a high hedge, regular trees and gentle water.

The side water entering the river along the way comes from the tailrace of Jordan's mill, for the central waterwheel no longer takes the full water flow. It is the outflow of the bypassing spillway, seen on the eastern side when you go and look at the mill – from this spot framed by a spread of trees. Before long, on this navigation section of the Ivel, the disused loading docks come into view on the other bank and the river narrows to something like 12' to 14'. Then on to the B658 at Holme with its scattering of houses.

Two things of interest before moving on. Firstly, go round on the road and take a look at the mill, made famous as the logo of Jordan's products and pay a visit sometime to their delightful epicurean shop. You cannot help but notice the other attraction across the grass, being the guillotine sluice built in 1967 by the Gt. Ouse River Authority at the disused lock, reminiscent of the times when the river conveyed working boats.

We take to the Broom road, passing the Grange – a name derived either from Cistercian farms managed by lay-brothers or, more generally, meaning granary or barn. The flat landscape to the south has punctuations of tree clumps and this proves a not unpleasant road walk. Shortly after passing the Gypsy Lane side road a view of Broom Hall can be spotted through the hedge, being an imposing red brick building. Further on, buildings converted into dwellings bear the names of Carriage, Bothy and Stables, and so on to the triangular shaped green, determined by the roads leaving on the Southill road.

Look for the B.W. sign at the end of a row of cottages, some thatched; this leads out into the field and passes on the north side of the Manor Farm buildings onto a very good made-up drive out onto the B658. Left for a short way and then use the substantial tractor width B.W. heading off west, a distance of only a few yards on the road. Out across the flat fields cultivated in small areas for a variety of crops, as will be discovered on both the Biggleswade walks, for this region does both arable farming and market gardening. Don't be put off by the fact that they hang their scarecrows on gibbets, nor be surprised by the giant irrigation sprays. This part of the walk proves to be a mile long on this stretch, with a patchwork of trees in a north/south alignment making what appears one continuous wood. Ultimately a road corner presents itself, where young trees have been planted as an enhancement. Then soon after on the road the green arrowed B.W. turns off on your right at a gateway, whilst a great woodland hiding a lake now occupies the southern side of the road.

Verges on this excellent stone track support a wealth of meadowland plants, poppies, sorrel, mixed grasses in profusion and a variety of flowers in the umbelliferous families. Trees in the covert alongside were planted 15–20 years ago as small saplings, for I remember them being planted. A dog-leg is encountered, so make sure you enter the field in front, crossing the bend in the track, then bear left and follow the tree-lined brook on a just about distinguishable path. This in turn joins a country road, an approach road for the Shuttleworth Agricultural College, and being in the vicinity of the Old Warden Airfield and Museum there is a chance that you might get a flying display, either by vintage aircraft or more likely by more humble flying models.

Go right now eastwards to Biggleswade on a beautifully 'manicured' edged roadway. (A bridleway going north at the rear of the airfield leaves the roadway, either for extra viewing or as an alternative way back to Biggleswade). We pass the exquisite lawns and firs of Kings Hall Farm, complete with willow-fringed pond, all providing a visual treat. Continue on until the road is met. Turn left by the cottages, where a general view of the area we are now leaving is gained, and leave on the next B.W. right, leading to Hill House.

The trees behind the house conceal a moat. On reaching a farm track 'tee' junction, pass over using the F.P. ahead, keeping in the same easterly direction through small interlinking cattle fields with either good tracks or paths, staying generally to the R.H. fence/hedgeline, noting that it can be muddy in places.

Now comes the tricky bit. Stay in the same east line and look for a section in the barbed-wired fencing alongside a water-filled ditch which has three telegraph poles for the bridge crossing. Cross the next narrow field bearing slightly right and be prepared for a fight with the nettles and elder at the stile in the banked hedgerow. (Not impassable, otherwise it would not be in this book – the more who walk this route the better for keeping it open, so do some cutting). Easy going now again, on a good stone track across the field in the direction of Biggleswade church tower. Cross the road, then down to Brooklands Farm, which has barn conversions at the rear in a clever development scheme, then round the bend towards the Biggleswade bypass. There's a drainage channel by the trees with a bridge, then the A1 must be confronted. Take care on this busy road, but the central barrier has a gap enabling a good crossing. A path crosses small fields, ash and willow lined, joining a bridleway beside watercourses, leading us back to the weir beside Biggleswade Mill and completing the walk.

Bird Protection

Places included: BIGGLESWADE – SANDY WARREN – POTTON – SUTTON

Length of walk: 8 miles.

Grid Ref: Sheet 153 202 463.

Parking: Either near the hospital or near the house called 'The Chequers' on the outskirts of Biggleswade on the Potton Road (B1040).

Bus services: 171, 176, 177 and 180.

Public Houses: The Bricklayer's Arms (Potton), John O'Gaunt (Sutton) and pubs in Biggleswade.

Walk Links: The B1040 into Biggleswade, then make for the church by the river for Walk 12.

Notes 1: The earthworks in the corner of the golf course at Sutton is supposed to be the site of John O'Gaunt's manor house.

BIRD PROTECTION

It was the wholesale slaughter of egrets, birds of paradise, kingfishers and many other species throughout the world for the feather fashion trade, worth several million pounds, that prompted Mrs. Robert Williamson to call a meeting on the subject. Mrs. Williamson, wife of a Manchester solicitor, had the meeting in her home in the February of 1889 for people sharing her concern. Thus came into being the Society for the Protection of Birds. Immediately they involved influential people under the Presidency of the Duchess of Portland. Nowadays people are similarly concerned about the killing of certain wild animals, especially the big cats, for their fur – ocelots, cheetahs and leopards, to name but a few.

In 1900 membership stood at 44,000, now in the 1990s the Society has 540,000 adults, whilst their Young Ornithologists Club boasts a further 10,700 members. At the turn of this century they were campaigning against the trapping of songbirds by pole-traps and the liming of roosting branches. About this time in Britain ospreys and white tailed eagles were near extinction, and a system of watching breeding sites was instituted. The Society realised that, though some nests could be guarded, the greater risk was that many of the habitats were being destoyed. This led to the decision

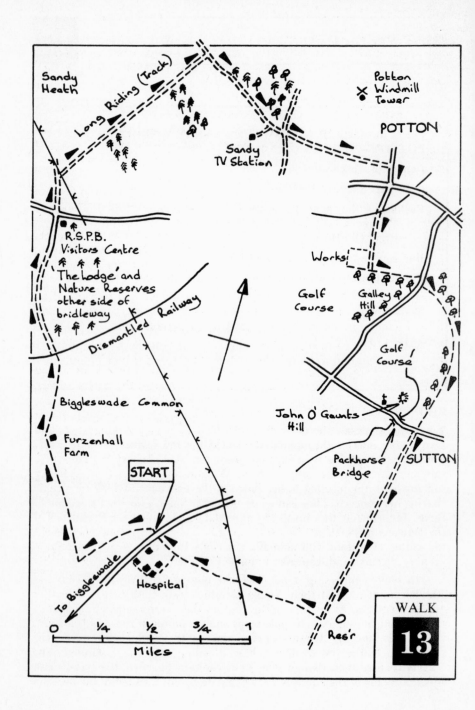

Sandy Heath

Long Riding (Track)

Potton Windmill Tower

POTTON

Sandy TV Station

R.S.P.B. Visitors Centre

'The Lodge' and Nature Reserves other side of bridleway

Dismantled Railway

Works

Golf Course

Galley Hill

Golf Course

Biggleswade Common

Furzenhall Farm

John O' Gaunts Hill

START

Packhorse Bridge

SUTTON

To Biggleswade

Hospital

Res'r

0   1/4   1/2   3/4   1
Miles

WALK
13

by the Society to purchase its first reserve at Romney Marsh in Kent, but because of land drainage nearby the wading birds disappeared. Undeterred, they acquired precarious sites or places of special significance, and now they manage 114 reserves covering 180,000 acres.

Bedfordshire comes into the story when in 1961 the Society moved its London headquarters into the former home of Viscount Peel, Speaker of the House of Commons. Sandy Lodge, built in the 1870's on Sandy Warren, has a 104-acre estate nature reserve set out with nature trails. From the headquarters a network of 11 regional offices was created to embrace the whole country.

Oil slicks and the resultant plight of seabirds and swans keep the Society's efforts in the press, while pesticides cause constant alarm along with other chemicals harmful for birdlife in the countryside. Then there is the indiscriminate killing of migratory birds, in many countries for the cage-bird trade, and the multitudinous deaths caused by the pursuit of eggs, particularly those of rare birds. Then there is also the dilemma of breeding, rearing and shooting pheasants for sport and as a means of income.

Success, and they do have many successes, might well be typified by their logo, that of the avocet, for, resulting from their efforts, this wading bird reintroduced itself in Minsmere where its particular habitat has been re-created. Ospreys and white tailed eagles are back under considerable supervision. Now the bittern, a member of the heron family with a peculiar booming call, has come under scrutiny. Requisite dyke management has led to the breeding of sufficient eels as the key staple food of the bittern, which was once a relatively common bird served at feast-time.

The very professionally produced colour magazine of the Society called 'Birds' gives ornithologists much encouragement and is naturally most informative on topical issues and bird profiles.

Possibly the best conclusion would be a quotation from the centenary article in the Spring 1989 issue of the Bedfordshire Magazine, written by the R.S.P.B. Press Officer, Chris Harbard.

'During the Society's evolution from a band of Victorian gentlewomen into the influential international conservation organisation of today, its aims have been relatively unchanged. The active protection of wild birds and the encouragement of people to take an interest in birds and the countryside have been the two major objectives. The support which the Society now gets from its half million members is not only financial but also vocal, and without it the R.S.P.B. would not be *the* organisation which takes action for wild birds and the environment.'

BIGGLESWADE – SANDY WARREN – POTTON – SUTTON

Cross the stile at the roadside and make your way round to the rear of the 'Chequers' house where a bridleway will be found. The good track passes greenhouses, and the holdings on the right have sections of flowers for the 'cut flower' market. Now we come onto a staggered bridleway junction with our direction right, parallel to the nearby railway. These fields get divided into onion growing plots, a crop which, along with Brussel sprouts, is a Bedfordshire speciality. We come onto Furzenhall Farm, an interesting composition in yellow brick, having corbelling coursed eaves, augmented by header brick string courses and 'fish-scale' tiling. (Furze = bracken etc. cut as fuel to fire kilns and brick clamps). By all appearances the building looks as if it was constructed as a vernacular 'hall' house. The once 'model' farm-yard buildings (see Book 1) look rather sorry for themselves.

A slight change of direction veering right through double gates, one after the other, making diagonally across this field towards a white barred gate, aiming for the second pylon on the wooded hill line. Actually the path is clearly formed, and in this area the break in the Greensand Ridge is most pronounced, caused by the R. Ivel breaking through. This flat area on the map bears the name Biggleswade Common.

After the gate cross the bridge over a drainage water-course into a wood of oaks and ferns, a definite sign of sandy soil, taking a gentle uphill gradient. Pass over the dismantled Potton railway, seen as a green ribbon with colonised banks, but this is a forbidden area. Keeping in the same northerly direction under the trees, we come upon the sandy perimeter drive outside the Warren grounds' walls. Through between the ironstone gateless pillars into the Nature Reserve grounds of Sandy Lodge. Now comes a sharp uphill walk through the mixed woodlands on a broad sandy way, making sure you do not stray into the area marked 'private woods'. Keep straight, ignoring the coloured arrows of the R.S.P.B. trails, following the R.H. wire fence. You'll be accompanied by the sound of birdsong and will notice quite a number of bird boxes in the trees. The broad path comes upon the entry road to the Lodge which is used. Rhododendrons, with Douglas and Scots pines amongst other species, make a wonderful selection of trees – one of the finest I have seen for variety. We are well and truly on the sand now.

Before leaving the grounds, take a look at the Swiss chalet-type visitors' reception building, called Bird Shop, blessed with overhanging eaves, cross-braced balconies and downward pointing finials on the pat-terned bargeboards. Why not take a look inside at the merchandise and discover the origins of the R.S.P.B., before departing?

Cross the Sandy – Potton road, still in a northward direction on the gravel drive marked by green arrows, up to the grid system pylon where you get a good effect in looking at the television mast through its lattice structure. Sharp R. on the B.W., making sure you do not go forward on this junction. Trees all about us, though not always near at hand, on this named Long Riding Track up on Sandy Heath. Leaving the fir tree belt the track passes through big fields, augmented with plantations which have their timbers cut into pit-prop sizes. The gravel drive makes for pleasant going, with only the television mast serving as a reminder of the 20th century and as an example of man's work up on the heath. After a straight stretch of about ¾ mile or more, an oak line appears in front, going out left onto the Sandy – Everton road. Turn R. here in a familiar mixed woodland, this time belonging to the Everton Estates; a really wonderful atmosphere in surroundings of filtered sunlight.

Those ardent watchers of T.V. programmes on woodland natural history will recognise the levels in woodland strata, starting with nettles and bracken ground cover, an interspersed intermediate level of shrubs (here hazels and brambles thrive), before meeting on our vertical scale the middle and upper branches of the trees. Prolific birdlife through these woods.

But be careful or you will miss seeing the base of the famous television mast; that giant latticed triangular structure carrying dishes and a pillar on top, held up by a great complex array of wired guys. Just after the T.V. station entrance and still in the woodland drive is a bend in the track and we come to a junction on a slope – take care for a moment. Don't go downhill on the road right nor slightly uphill left side, as this goes into private grounds and strawberry fields. Go straight over, taking the narrow B.W. sign for Old Bedford Road. The stony path develops into a sandy track through cultivated plots, overlooked by the stump of poor old Potton windmill tower. Past the glasshouses into Old Bedford Road, then, at the crossroads in the houses, right down Newtown, coming upon the Bricklayers Arms P.H. on the Sandy road B1042. Cross, continuing down Sutton Mill Road (which has houses on both sides) before coming to a rough road, after crossing the bed of the Potton railway.

The route is increasingly becoming rural in the vicinity of the Sewage Farm. On meeting the tree-line edging the golf course, go left on the perimeter path, proceeding east under trees, through spruce plantings, before coming upon the road at the gates. Cross the road in a right diagonal, seeking a F.P. sign almost hidden in the high hedges, venturing now on an open woodland walk with spread out trees. Still beside the golf course the path is defined by a row of planted quicksets, which in the course of time will become a shrouding fence for the golfing fraternity. A bridge over a drainage channel, then diagonally R. on a well walked path through the corn, crossing a second bridge. The path now follows the crop edge (depends on the seasons) beside the golf course tree plantations along their fairway extremities, and signs are that people choose to walk amongst the young trees. Anyway, the field L. is of major proportions, the far side being out of sight, and when the woodland border of the golf course turns away we come upon a green grass path into Sutton. But before leaving this position look through the hedgerow for the earthworks of John O'Gaunt hill. Needless to say, the pub in Sutton is called 'John O'Gaunt' and the village possesses a notable packhorse bridge on the western side which would make an interesting diversion.

Opposite where the path enters Sutton across the road leaves our exit – a broad bridleway, stretching straight for a good mile south out into the flat countryside, through vast cornfields broken only by intermittent odd trees. The way eventually enters a short stretch of a remnant green lane, with a watercourse going under in a culvert. Go on a little way then turn right onto a main field access B.W. Away on the left West Sunderland Farm stands alone in the fields.

The surface becomes gravel on this ½ mile stretch, then on reaching the grid system against the hedge go right for about 75 yards by a brook. Look for a bridge and stile bringing you out into a field with many scattered high bushes. This becomes the last stage and for preference keep by the L.H. hedge; cows are likely to be in this field so don't be surprised. Stay in this field, ignoring the stile in the corner, and follow round, making for the single-storey yellow brick and red tiled house. Staying by the hedge the road gateway comes into view, completing this circular walk.

British Farming

Places included: WRESTLINGWORTH – HATLEY ST. GEORGE AND COCKAYNE HATLEY AREA

Length of walk: 7¼ miles (see Notes).

Grid Ref: Sheet 153 259 477.

Parking: At the church just off the through road in Wrestlingworth up the one-way road marked for the church.

Bus services: 173, 174 and 175 (all Biggleswade buses).

Public Houses: The Chequers and Queen Victoria (Wrestlingworth).

Walk Links: Roads from Wrestlingworth and Cockayne Hatley go to Potton for Walk 13.

Notes 1: This part of Bedfordshire gets largely ignored by ramblers and should be used more often. It's somewhat lonely here and one needs to be a hardy walker. One is rewarded by extensive views across East Bedfordshire and South Cambridgeshire, and it makes an alternative to walking the Gamlingay end of the Greensand Ridge Walk.

2: An alternative return for the walk can be made by the bridleway between Cockayne Hatley and Potton Woods and minor roads, making an anti-clockwise walk. (Left out of Hatley Park for this alternative).

3: Variations. A linear walk can be made using bridleways from Biggleswade through to Wrestlingworth.
For the long-distance walker starting from Biggleswade, go to Wrestlingworth, then East Hatley and A.C.W. Hatley St. George, Cockayne Hatley Wood, on to Potton and return either via Sutton (20 miles) or Sandy Heath (22 miles) into Biggleswade.

BRITISH FARMING

A small profile of British farming seems appropriate in a book of this sort, since the reader will gain first-hand experience on visiting the countryside. 250,000 farms with 400,000 farmers are reckoned to be in the United Kingdom, taking up 17 million hectares, farms being so mechanised that they no longer have the large 'armies' of workers. Even so, 7,000 workers

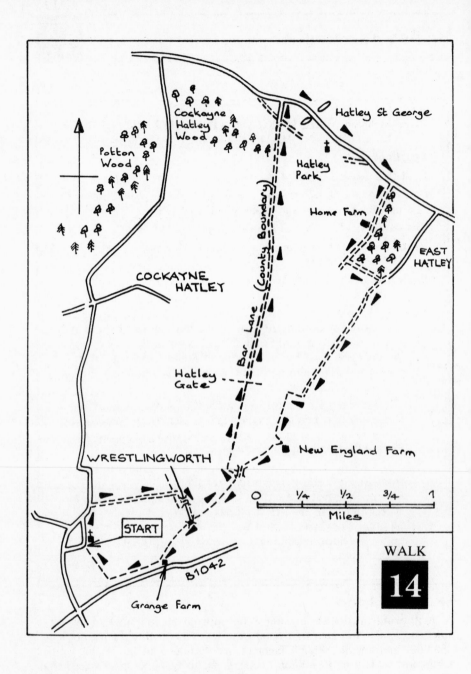

Potton Wood

Cockayne Hatley Wood

Hatley St George

Hatley Park

Home Farm

EAST HATLEY

COCKAYNE HATLEY

Bar Lane (County Boundary)

Hatley Gate

WRESTLINGWORTH

New England Farm

START

B1042

Grange Farm

0   ¼   ½   ¾   1
Miles

WALK

14

80

left the land in one year because of the surpluses. These surpluses, according to articles in journals, are on the decline in Europe; however, money must be spent on just keeping food in store – refrigerated, where necessary.

Something like 1.35 million hectares of land may no longer be needed for agriculture by the mid-1990s, consequently one hears alternative land usage being mooted. This complex situation, bound by strong rules, could mean areas of land being 'set aside' under payment schemes or, in a non-intensive utilisation capacity, we may see more reprieves for meadowland or even such areas re-created. Also one finds more land planted with trees, and a case can be made for national self-sufficiency in timber not only for structural and furniture making purposes but also for paper production. Our native deciduous trees should be planted whenever possible, both by the Forestry Commission and the private landowner, satisfying replenishment and visual pleasure at the same time.

Old farm buildings present less of a problem in finding new uses rather than their demolition, and as they are usually substantially built it makes them prime candidates for conversion into dwellings.

Currently issued figures for the U.K. show 12 million cattle, 40 million sheep, 8 million pigs and 131 million chickens, whilst 15,000 million litres of milk and 12,000 million eggs are consumed nationally per annum.

As background reading for this second book of walks, the writer has been reading 'Farmers Weekly' and would recommend other countryside lovers to do likewise, though bearing in mind that, like all professional journals, the contributors tend to wear 'rose tinted spectacles'. What should fascinate readers is the range and breadth of the articles, even admonishments for the over-use of nitrates or for over-enthusiastic hedge-grubbing. Country users tend only to read the conservation magazine articles or the 'glossies' disregarding the practitioners' own weekly.

One finds all the livestock sales totalised and valued weekly, plus an extensive advertisement section from working farm sales through to protective clothing, taking in job vacancies, farm equipment and livestock sales on the way. Amongst the small 'ads' appear 'introduction services', a reflection on the sort of isolated lives they lead; a number of farmers advertise, giving a profile of themselves, seeking friendships leading to marriages!

Not unexpectedly you will find numerous articles on livestock, crop yields, rearing methods, county shows and farming equipment. As a sign of the times, refurbished machines are making a comeback, such that a recent £20,000 tractor can be bought for half price or less, for instance.

WRESTLINGWORTH – HATLEY ST. GEORGE AND COCKAYNE HATLEY AREA

Spare a look at the church here, for remarkably this is built with pebbles with stone dressings, a neat compact building with a suitably proportioned tower. Something of merit can be said about all of Bedfordshire's older churches encountered on these walks.

Set off north, away from the church, down the narrow Church Lane, joining the through road opposite Brookside Garage and go right in the direction of Cockayne Hatley. Braggs Lane comes just after the Queen Victoria P.H.; a signposted B.W. leaves the end of this lane with its very desirable residences in their own grounds. A high windbreaking hedge gives protection and the track surface is firm; a drainage ditch bridge marks the end of the shelter. Go on into the corner of the arable field and make your way round to the B.W. post. This stands at a ditch crossing which is used. Now follow the same ditch to the high tree line ahead, where another ditch appears in front of the trees. Since these are very deep (man height, for I saw them scraped out) you do not want to be on the wrong side. A change of direction north-east and for a good distance, 1½ miles actually, we shall be on the county boundary with Cambridgeshire. After a small change in direction in the field corner, where a bridge brings the return of this walk, we leave the tree belt and go due north on a long haul in open fields. Only the Sandy mast provides a recognisable landmark; no buildings except for the New England Farm, and not a car in sight here.

However, the distant trees are the spur across this openness, coming onto Hatley Gate, which in reality is found to be a field crossing on the end of Bar Lane. A gap in the hedge takes you into the next great field, but before doing so turn around and take in the huge vista of eastern Bedfordshire – quite a reward, which will be seen mostly on the return. Bar Lane is a designated ancient track, now grown across mostly, but we use the broad grass swathe on the R.H.S., still the county boundary. In fact the track will go into the tree line, so take advantage as it harbours wild flowers, and the fallen decayed timber is colonised by fungi and insects. (Several side-tracks go out across the fields; they cannot be used and are marked 'private').

The great mass of Cockayne Hatley Wood abuts the walk; it is almost an extension of Potton Wood and here the county boundary turns along the edge of these woods. A different scenery emerges, that of parkland beside a broad avenue which we find outselves on, between woodland, for this is horse-rearing country of poplar lined, railed corrals and several stable blocks. The outside of a walled garden adds to the visual interest, with potting sheds inside and lean-to glasshouses reminding one of the B.B.C T.V. series on the Victorian walled kitchen garden. Cross the chestnut avenue still on a track north then through two lots of gates onto the road.

For this walk we turn right, which will prove more interesting than at first glance seems likely. For one thing Gamlingay can be seen two miles away, the termination of Bedfordshire's Greensand Ridge Walk, and as an extra a glimpse of Cambridgeshire's scenery. Then, reaching the bend on the way to the church of Hatley St. George, a row of ponds straddles the road, where there are very good chances of seeing heron, especially the one on the left side. (I saw a dozen wading and fishing and getting up to do the odd bit of flying – amazing). The low elevation of the red brick Park House, with a white turreted, creeper-clad stable block and outbuildings augmenting the principal building, makes a visual backdrop for the grazing cattle in the foreground. A pastoral setting very much a man-made creation but none the worse for that.

The plain but nicely proportioned church stands on a grassy rise by the road, surrounded by the obligatory yews, whilst on the other side of the road the Church Farm buildings around two yards have been converted into workshops for all sorts of occupations, as can be read on the entry name-board. An admirable utilisation of property – see the rural industries notes in this book – better than demolition whilst retaining the character in their mix of Cambridgeshire yellow lime bricks contrasted with terracotta coloured string courses. A few fine detached residences look out across the woods and onto the village green, and now keep your eyes open for the Home Farm entrance road opposite the Post Office. Everything is called Hatley hereabouts, though we don't go to East Hatley, and out of interest a look at the O.S. map shows many moats in this area. (A subject written on in Book 1 for South Bedfordshire).

A good tarmac road past the great farm complex – even a grain drying facility – and then onto a stone track beside the thick wood, turning left on the corner up to the top of the rise. A plain building here could be for aircraft, as evidenced by the wind-sock nearby, and the broad stretches of grass are quite suitable for landings.

Although not visible, the A14 runs nearby between Royston and Huntingdon, being the ancient Ermine Street, whilst further over in the east are hills beyond Royston, the vale being the course of the River Cam. Southwards the extensive view sweeps out across north Hertfordshire and east Bedfordshire from a height of 75 m. (230 ft.).

A change of direction south on an excellent stone track beside a mixed shrub shelter hedge. No trees and few hedges in these almost inhumanly scaled fields, and in East Anglia proper they are often bigger still. In places in this hedge the tree-planting message seems to be getting a chance, and after a while we find ourselves walking on grass. When the hedge halts go right around the corner (the B.W. skirting New England Farm is now

83

totally missing), cross the ditch on the concrete pipe provided and make a left turn by the ditch in the corner. The poor trees, fallen and decaying, seem blighted; the lack of re-planting looks a frightful error for this pocket copse, especially as it is the alignment with Hatley Gate.

Stay in the field i.e. ditch on your right, and go down the field access track for the isolated farm, then change direction for Wrestlingworth, following the R.H.S. of a watercourse ditch down to the tree line of the outgoing walk, where a bridge makes the connection. Retrace your footsteps right the way round to the end of the long hedged B.W. coming out of Braggs Lane, stopping at the bridge. You now have a choice of returning on the same route or making a 'back door' entry into the village.

For the latter go on the Wrestlingworth side of the left watercourse and return to our inescapable tree and ditchline. (The locals might know an avoiding alternative through the hedges – see sketch map). This will bring you out to Grange Farm on the road. Don't go through the farmyard, but enter the narrow field, with wood and farm equipment lying about, and go in the direction of Wrestlingworth.

The paths go close by the stream, and, when nearer, a diagonal direction up the slope to the church can be taken, leaving the field by a 'kissing gate'.

Bedfordshire's Rural Industries

Places included: SHEFFORD – CLIFTON – LANGFORD

Length of walk: 7¾ miles.

Grid Ref: Sheet 153 143 393.

Parking: Public car parks or dispersal parking in Shefford.

Bus services: 181 and 182.

Public Houses: White Swan and others in Shefford. Dun Cow (Langford). Green Man (Stanford).

Walk Links: This walk can be added to the end of Walk 16. A road link can be made through Southill into Old Warden meeting Walk 11; also, using the Stanford to Broom road brings you out onto Walk 12; alternatively one could go through Southill.

Notes 1: A pleasant circular that can be done in either direction, with good views out over the R. Ivel valley besides walking alongside the waters.

BEDFORDSHIRE'S RURAL INDUSTRIES

The variety of rural industries can come as a shock for those assuming that only potters and corn-dolly makers work in rural workshops these days. High technology, precision engineering, electronics, defence projects and medical industries are out there in the countryside, besides computing agencies, sub-contract, building products, as exampled by the Faldo Industrial estate at Barton-in-the-Clay.

Discounting the purely agricultural and allied trades, one expects there are a host that will come as no real surprise in Bedfordshire. Among business products and services we find angling tackle, fencing, fertilisers, fireplaces, food products, furniture, game-breeding, horses, horticulture, land-drainage, leaded and stained glass manufacture. Then there come maltsters, millers, name-plate makers, organ builders, printers, quarryers, mat makers, steeplejacks, stonemasons, timber merchants and vine keepers. And this list did not include those engaged in the arts and crafts fields of activities.

The Rural Development Commission, which succeeded CoSIRA, has 30,000 small firms on its books employing 116,000 people throughout England. It grew as an organisation out of the Rural Industries Bureau

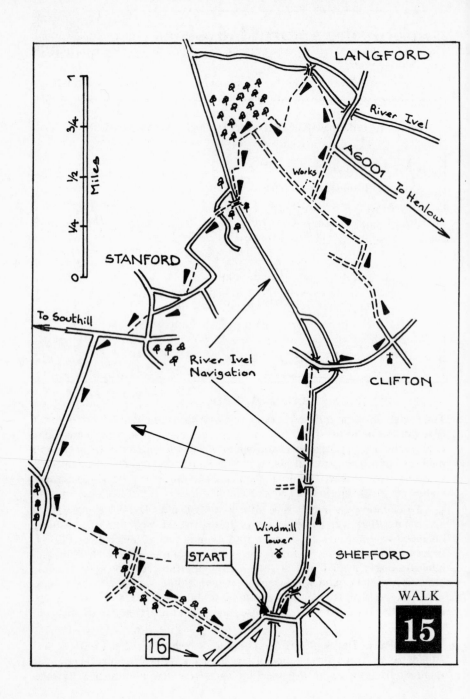

LANGFORD

River Ivel

A6001 To Henlow

Works

STANFORD

To Southill

River Ivel Navigation

CLIFTON

Miles

1
3/4
1/2
1/4
0

Windmill Tower

START

SHEFFORD

16

WALK

15

founded in 1923. The Commission's intentions remain unchanged since that year, i.e. to support and encourage small businesses to form the backbone of rural employment.

Rural enterprises obtain free of charge, or heavily subsidised, advisory services from the Commission for those employing 20 or less, providing they meet certain criteria. Expert advice includes accountancy, commerce, marketing etc., besides specialist expertise as required for ceramics, plastics, saw-milling, thatching, woodworking and building work.

Much of the available money goes on creating premises and the conversion of redundant rural buildings, for the supply of suitable accommodation is a constant handicap. Derelict buildings come under their scrutiny to ascertain their potential.

A look at the name-boards at the entrance to the light industrial estates springing up on the outskirts of small to medium-sized villages and towns gives some indication of the diversity of manufacture and services on offer. Enterprises turn up in some of the most out of the way places. Really this upsurge has only been possible because of electricity and the 'work-horse' of so many industrial operations, the fractional horsepower motor.

WALK

15

SHEFFORD – CLIFTON – LANGFORD

Our circular walk taking in Langford starts from the bridge over the R. Flit, where the White Swan P.H. stands on the north bank in the large village of Shefford. However, on the south bank, a F.P. sign indicates the path, which is quite narrow under a canopy of trees, whilst on the other side gardens sweep down to the water's edge. Round the bend a nameless tributary is encountered, bringing waters from the Gravenhurst area, and crossed by an arched iron bridge taking the path in a straight line, rejoining the river in the River Ivel Navigation section. Over on the northern side stands the tower of the Shefford windmill, whilst at our other side we have a drainage brook for company.

This section of the river (and another stretch met on the return of the walk) typifies the canalisation of rivers, making them navigable for the boat traffic preceding the age of canal-building proper. Thus, hauled barges supplied towns like Shefford with coal and goods, then carrying away local produce. When the field access bridge is met a ¼ mile or so along the bank, cross the navigation, continuing in the same direction on the path trodden out on the overgrown banks. Teazles grow in these quarters, reeds wave their fronds in the breezes and the river weeds stir in the currents.

Continue up onto the road, bearing right, which crosses the old navigation course and the river meanders in an area where willows, poplars, sycamores, evergreens and other trees flourish in the damp soils. Up into Clifton village, having passed the cricket field and spared a glance up at the church. Left at the crossroads, walking beside a terrace of red brick string course model cottages – model because almost certainly built in the era of farm improvements some 100–200 years ago.

On leaving the last houses the substantial surfaced lane heads out into the fields, with the Iver Navigation discernable not so far away. Stay on the way, which brings us up to a solitary barn/garage; left here, using the footpath through the large flat fields which skirt the boundary fence of the sewerage works. Turn sharp right on the southern side onto a trackway crossing a brook, and then between hedges out onto the bend of the A6001 coming from Henlow, which can be very busy.

Carry on forward in an easterly direction, watching out for an entry into a field marked by a F.P. sign. The gateway is none too strong but leads into a field with rather a lot of nettle clumps. Go alongside the L.H. for about 100 yards and then change direction, making for the red brick house with a white balcony in the distance. A reasonable pathway can be found in this rough horse-grazing field by keeping on the western side following another watercourse, for this is the coming from the direction of Hitchin. The river is relatively broad here by the houses and has a resident duck population; cross the bridge and enjoy the setting on the seats under the trees or go into Langford for a pub stop.

We now have several choices. a/ complete the circular, b/ return along the same route or c/ get a lift.

To continue, leave Langford by re-crossing the river at the same spot, but this time walk away directly from the river, bearing very slightly right, negotiating the wet ground on a winding path of sorts. There is a stile in the boundary hedge, so enter the next field and follow the L.H. hedgrow in a direction away from Langford; this should be a well-trodden path. The path passes the end of a farm lane, bringing the walker into the field's corner by a ditch; clockwise here and continue up to the wood on the other side. Cross at the footbridge and skirt the side of the wood (though the map shows the path on the inside) – no matter. After passing the access bridleway coming up from the sewerage works, a field boundary stream is met at the extremity of neighbouring woodland. This is followed, turning westwards, then halfway to the next clump of trees a sturdy footbridge is encountered and used, then walk up to end of this wedge-shaped field under the trees, as this is the correct right of way.

Before crossing the River Ivel Navigation notice how straight the stretches in both directions are, illustrating the 'cuts' made by 'navvies' (derived from the term 'inland navigators' i.e. canal-constructors). The map shows the Navigation joining the R. Ivel beyond the last wood. So up the slope and join the minor road for Stanford, observing that in this area houses have distinctive terracotta red 'roman' tiled roofs. The diagonal path right, just beyond the first bend, is worth taking, marked by a F.P. sign, then take the left fork up to the road tee junction.

Ahead stands an old house beside a high hedge where the departing path threads through (none too obvious), then diagonally cross a cultivated field just above the Green Man P.H., ending out on the Southill road. Shortly a side road comes into view heading west, which is part of the route involving something like a mile of road walking which cannot be helped, as the Ordnance Survey map confirms. Southill Park woods bound a road into Southill and a track coming from the fields on the left may be noticed but not used. Go on a bit further, some 200 yards, and a F.P. sign in the hedgerow should be discovered.

Stay on the L.H.S. of the hedge bank, which after a while means we are alongside a small copse, travelling in a southerly direction. Then comes a field access trackway on the corner of the copse; go ahead and bear right on this new course. Yet another change of direction after a short distance, when the tree belt(s) climbing up from the road is joined. Before descending, good views should be obtained from this high ground, though they can be obscured by mists. A gentle downhill stroll lies in front on this well-surfaced bridleway, for it is used as such, and so out onto the Shefford–Bedford road, the A600.

Needless to say, this is the return by turning left on this road, but, before doing so, notice the high bank in this vicinity which is the bed of the dismantled Henlow to Bedford railway line coming from Hitchin, now taken over by natural colonising. Ignore the B658 at the tee junction just north of the river.

Bedfordshire's Airships II – The Phoenix Briefly Arises

Places included: ELSTOW – HAYNES – SHEFFORD

Length of walk: 7¾ miles.

Grid Ref: Sheet 153 053 468.

Parking: Medbury Lane off Pear Tree Lane. (This is a linear walk so return arrangements must be made, or alight here and make transport connections at the other end).

Bus services: X1, X2, X3, X4, X50, X51 and X52.

Public Houses: The Rose (Littleworth), The Greyhound (Haynes, Northwood End Road) and pubs in Elstow and Shefford.

Walk Links: Walks 15 and 16 can be combined as the bridge over the River Ivel in Shefford is common to both walks. Connections can be made through Harrowden and Cardington for Cople on Walk 10.

Notes 1: This is the only linear walk in the book as is the Upper Lea Valley walk in Book 1. Alternative views of the airship sheds are gained on this walk.

2: Rowney Warren, fringed near the end of the walk, contains forest walks ideal for a short future outing with children, introducing them to the countryside.

3: Chicksands Priory is within the U.S.A.F. camp written about in several Bedfordshire books. The great circular early warning aerial, all pervading, will not be found on O.S. maps.

BEDFORDSHIRE'S AIRSHIPS II – THE PHOENIX BRIEFLY RISES

There will always be advocates for the concept of lighter than air dirigible craft, for there are only five ways of being airborne viz. aircraft, helicopters, airships, gliders and balloons. The latter two must be discounted as a means of general travel for obvious reasons, whilst the third option these days has come under closer scrutiny and is the subject of considerable research.

Books on airships reveal that an impressive total mileage was clocked up prior to their demise in Europe and the U.S., though the latter never gave up their use in submarine detection work and coastal duties. Airships could cruise at 70 m.p.h. with passengers enjoying spacious saloons as on

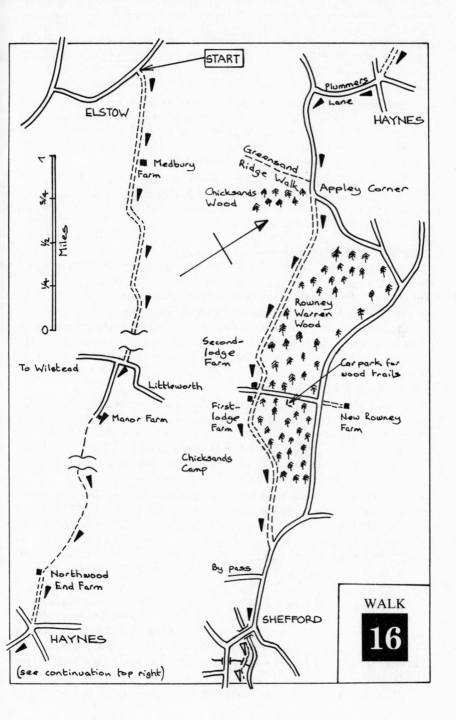

START

ELSTOW

Plummers
Lane

HAYNES

Medbury
Farm

Greensand
Ridge Walk

Chicksands
Wood

Appley Corner

Miles

1

3/4

1/2

1/4

0

Rowney
Warren
Wood

Second-
lodge
Farm

Car park for
wood trails

To Wilstead

Littleworth

Manor Farm

First-
lodge
Farm

New Rowney
Farm

Chicksands
Camp

Northwood
End Farm

By pass

HAYNES

SHEFFORD

WALK

16

(see continuation top right)

91

cruise liners, sitting on lightweight cane furniture. However, these airships required large ground crews on the mooring ropes and they needed a lot of space for manoeuvring. They were in the main under-powered, for strong gales could drive them off course and rip the covering fabric.

In the 1970s researcher John Wood and naval architect Roger Munk re-thought the possibilities of airships using natural gas, whilst across the Atlantic the U.S. were considering using them as 'sky lifts' as an alternative to barge transportation of space rocket shells. They realised that airships required a re-assessment and that airships had potential.

After much anguish in solving almost insurmountable problems, their first new generation saw the light of day in Spring 1978, built using entirely new principles and materials. If it had not been for their dedicated team of workers, as chronicled in the B.B.C. T.V. documentary "The Half Million Pound Magic Carpet" about the Airship Developments, AD500 would not have got through her gestation, all the finance having been used up. Five weeks onwards, the AD500 having proved herself generally airworthy, she was destroyed by a gale. Two years later, under the auspices of Airship Industries a new airship of a similar capacity made its maiden flight, to be followed not long afterwards by the larger Skyship 600.

This new family of non-rigid airships uses coated polyester envelopes. Two air ballonets in the bottom of the envelope act as displacement airbags, maintaining the pressure and trim of the envelope with changes in atmospheric pressure and altitude. Kevlar cables hanging from arches inside the balloon carry the plastic gondola.

Power plant for the airship comprises two Porsche six-cylinder air-cooled piston engines of 204 h.p. for the 500 series and 255 h.p. turbo-charged versions for the 600 series. These engines, mounted in the rear of the gondola, each drive ducted five-bladed propellers with a facility for angular rotation, enabling 90° upward and 120° downward thrust. These vectored forces enable hover and VTOL capabilities.

Skyship 500 has a balloon length of 50 metres (152 ft.) and a 15 metres (50 ft.) diameter, carrying 7 passengers, whilst the 59 metres (193 ft.) long 15 metres (50 ft.) diameter envelope of the Skyship 600 accommodates 13 passengers, both ships making 50 knots. Their applications include city sightseeing tours, monitoring, search and retrieve with winched rescue boats, early warning capabilities and advertising, either by day or night using illuminated advertising banners.

Their almost nil radar signature makes them ideal for monitoring, and it is this feature that was destined to be fully exploited in the projected Sentinel 5000. The balloon would have housed a huge radar antenna for a wide range of military applications. With its double-decked gondola for the 12-man crew this airship would have been the largest non-rigid airship ever constructed.

However, in 1990 Airship Industries went into liquidation, bringing an end to airship construction work for a second time, with only some experimental meteorological balloon work remaining as a vestige of the past at Cardington.

Today the airship sheds find a very prosaic use with the No. 1 shed nearest Harrowden storing motor vehicles and the No. 2 shed used for fire and building research. The Shorts headquarters building faces an uncertain future, whilst in the larger building to the rear restoration work for the R.A.F. museum at Hendon is undertaken.

Airship interest at Cardington is kept alive by the Friends of the Cardington Airship Station (FOCAS) who ultimately want to establish a museum here depicting the working airship station.

WALK

16

ELSTOW – HAYNES – SHEFFORD

Medbury Lane skirts the edge of a small housing estate, before striking out into the fields as a made-up road, and for some time to come we shall be overshadowed by the giant airship hangars of Cardington.

Good to see tree-planting around the stream when we cross it by road bridge and follow the line of chestnut trees up to the yellow brick, 'E'-shaped Medbury Farm. Continuing on a raised track through earthwork ridges, the signs of mediaeval field systems, into a 'Z' bend by a corner barn. The bridleway now makes for the distant Haynes hill line, standing to a height of 91 metres (1,000ft.), going into the fields through a cattle-grid. Remnant hedges beside drainage ditches scatter the open fields as we walk now on a good stony track. Not far off we gain the impressive end view of the hangars.

The straight way reverts into a grass lane, with hedges and ditches on one side or another, gaining the road by means of a gravel drive. We turn right on the Wilstead road (left up the road on the bend stands 'The Rose' P.H.), then by the row of cottages turn into Elm Lane minor road, staying on this road right up to Manor Farm. A plaque dates the restoration as 1911 and the building has a pebbledash finish. There's a variety of materials used over the centuries in the range of barns, and going through the yard we pass a typical vernacular waggon-shed of a post and brace construction.

Leave the farm precinct on a stone-surfaced B.W. for the nearby wooded and field-capped hills, following a row of my beloved oaks in a retained hedge with the inclusion of some ash trees; it seems that most of the hedges exist hereabouts. Eventually we go through an iron gate followed by a wooden one 150 yards further on. Uphill now beside the L.H. hedge curving our way over the crest; from this vantage point look rearwards for views out over the Bedford region.

The path crosses arable fields to Northwood End Farm and its shelter-belt of planted trees. This B.W. does not now meet an unfenced road as shown on the O.S. map, as grass has been set across the route, but pass over all the same. In front of the immaculate farm stands a timber-framed granary barn on staddlestones, a most unusual feature, another example of which stands in the Chiltern Open Air Museum, re-erected from Wing, Bucks. Down the road into Haynes, which keeps its Festival of Britain name-board. One look at the O.S. map shows that Haynes has many 'ends'.

Stay on this road of bungalows called Plummer's Lane, being our exit out of Haynes, and the second landmark for this walk makes its appearance. We now see the giant early-warning-system circular aerial on the next hill line at Chicksands, but you won't see it on the O.S. map – as usual with sensitive military establishments. Descending down this country road are tiered cottages on the hillside, mostly thatched, all of them with very individual characteristics, the epitome of rural dwellings. On reaching the 'T' road junction turn left toward Chicksands Wood, and it is along this road that we meet up with the G.R.W. which follows this road for a short distance. Reaching Appley Corner this walk leaves the road on the bend, and utilises the concrete bridleway ahead.

The fields in this area are noted for their onion growing, then passing over the crest the byway follows the edge of Rowney Warren. Here a land irrigation plant and pond will be found, very possibly a giant hose-reel in the vicinity. At First Lodge Farm the back road into Chicksands Camp must be crossed. This road has the Rowney Warren car park, a good setting off point for the forest trails which are way-marked and ideal for short excursions. Instead of concrete we now have a sandy track beside the woods under the overhanging oaks, but the atmosphere is diminished somewhat by the presence of the R.A.F. camp not that far away across two fields. Leaving the wood boundary we meet the Shefford by-pass and the A600 main road, and now down the road into Shefford.

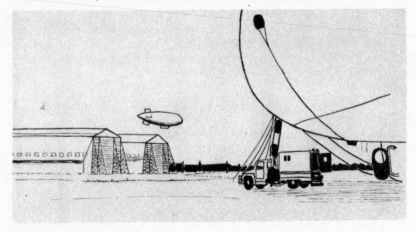

Mapping Where You Live

Places included: AMPTHILL – HOUGHTON CONQUEST

Length of walk: 4½ miles.

Grid Ref: Sheet 153 037 392.

Parking: Use the Houghton House car park; take care in turning off the dangerous bend on the Bedford road.

Bus service: 142, 143 and 145.

Public Houses: The Chequers on B530 out of Ampthill, and pubs in Ampthill.

Walk Links: Across the road and into Ampthill Park, joining up with Walk 18. These two walks combined make three loops.

Notes 1: The ruin of Houghton House must be visited as part of this walk, having associations with the Tudor Sydney family.

2: Kings Wood has great importance for botanists, so do be careful in this fragile habitat.

MAPPING WHERE YOU LIVE

Can you remember the ponds and all the farms in your parish? Unlikely, for few ponds survive and, particularly in the south of Bedfordshire, many farms are now under housing estates. Which brings us to the aim of this theme, which is basically recording for posterity. People need to know their past and where they live in relationship to the rest of the world; many a war has been fought on this very subject!

Local knowledge can be recorded by those other than local historians and archaeologists, for everyone has some local knowledge. Without local knowledge you would not be able to find your place of work! Placing our vote in elections not only involves the present generation and the parish as a unit of area, but also, by our concern and interest, forms a foundation for the future.

'Parish Maps' and 'The Parish Boundary', publications by an organisation called Common Ground, explore these wide-ranging topics in depth. Each of us remembers particular things and hears the recollections of older inhabitants. The lanes, animals in small fields, where children played, all these spring to mind, certainly they do for me, and we should take steps to record this knowledge. This information falls outside the remit of the

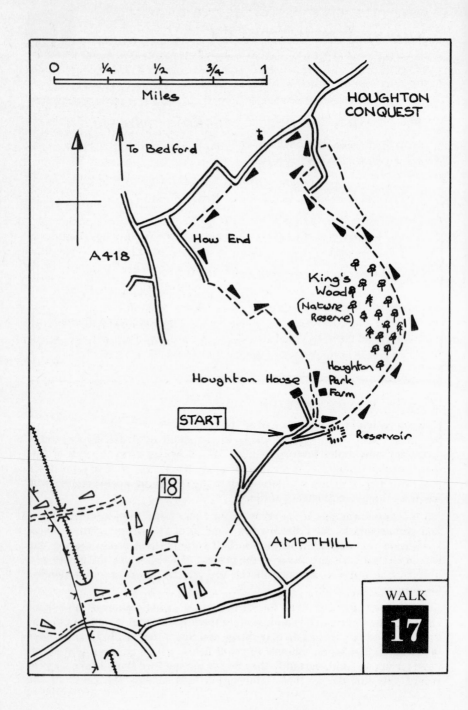

O ¼ ½ ¾ 1
Miles

To Bedford

HOUGHTON
CONQUEST

A418

How End

King's
Wood
(Nature
Reserve)

Houghton House

Houghton
Park
Farm

START

Reservoir

18

AMPTHILL

WALK

17

96

Ordnance Survey and, come to that, outside most social historians' writings. A pictorial representation of a small area speaks mountains. If all parishes or small neighbourhoods produced a parish or a town map – and quite a number have already done so – it would be most valuable.

"The important thing to aim for is something that people want and which reflects what they value about their place" states Tom Greaves, the author, and he goes on to say "Maps can show features that people love now or those they would miss if they were no longer there". So a 'map' can depict a given territory with changes over the course of time, e.g. the impact of canals, railways and new roads, or reflect a place at a given point in time, e.g. the heyday of lace-making and where all the lace-makers lived in a given locality.

Instead of a map as such, the final product can be a big picture of a place, say the Harrold/Odell/Felmersham gravel pits in the north-west of the county, and the big chalk pit centre of cement production at Houghton Regis, both in their way having a huge impact on nearby places. This approach of pictorial representation has been done in several parts of the country. Pictures of men working, the machinery involved, the kilns, all included in a montage, together with border pictures of all the species of wildlife now adopting the habitat make up one form of parish map. This can be extended to give a map of the working area and a diagram of where the products are sent and used round the world. Someone with artistic flair can marry up all the information, thus making a pleasing composition, but above all the end product must make a forceful statement, saying in so many words 'this is us at a given point in our history'.

Alternatively, old spellings of place names and 'potted' histories of familiar buildings can be inserted in a shape representing the parish boundary. Boundaries were once more important than they are today, as they defined the area of parish relief for the poor and the area under the 'management' of the local workhouse. As a serf you could be punished if you 'fled' from your parish, for the parishes did not want to look after other parishes' poor. Old field names, footpaths and byeways make another subject, and yet others can be devised as the two books describe. Also, there is no reason why a series of parish maps should not be produced for a village as different aspects get explored – get it recorded for posterity before everyone forgets.

Even applique or patchwork and embroidery have been used, for these 'maps' make wall-hangings in village halls; then there could be painted and fired tiles, sculpture and coloured cardboard models, painted or stained glass panels.

Who can make a 'map'? Well, the answer has got to be everybody, either individuals doing it all themselves or channelling information from multitudinous sources to a leader for a group effort by organisation, club or

Who can make a 'map'? Well, the answer has got to be everybody, either individuals doing it all themselves or channelling information from multitudinous sources to a leader for a group effort by organisation, club or evening class. What's holding you back from getting started?

Further information available from Bedfordshire Rural Community Council, The Old School, Cardington, Bedford, MK44 3SX.

AMPTHILL – HOUGHTON CONQUEST

The ruin of Houghton House sits below the crest of the ridge, so does not appear as a silhouette from a distance. Since the walk only passes alongside, it is best to pay the site a visit now, approaching down its gravel drive.

Leaving the visitors' car park, we use the same approach road in front of four terraced houses, but at their end turn sharp right on a curving track just before the large barns. This leads towards Kings Wood; occupying the middle distance views nearby is a grass covered water reservoir. From here Stewartby lake, Bedford and the famous pair of Cardington Airship hangars built by the R.A.F. for the R100 and the ill-fated R101 are clearly seen beyond these sheep-grazed slopes.

Kings Wood is a piece of ancient woodland with a flora habitat reckoned to have an ancestry dating as far back as the last Ice Age. This precious S.S.S.I. (Site of special scientific interest) is under the care of Bedfordshire County Council and the natural processes continue. Either take the G.R.W. path on a public right of way following the edge of the wood or the inside path. In choosing the latter have the utmost care, abiding strictly by the Country Code, and on no account leave the path; dogs definitely on a lead. Regeneration is visible in all directions, as trees fall and rot away and the replacement saplings gain strength. The rotten trunks are part of the food chain that include mosses and insects, all precariously balanced for survival, especially so in this technocratic 20th century.

In the wood we descend the contours, curving our way out at the bottom edge of this 'leg of mutton' shaped wood. This path, nearly a mile long, really is one of the most wonderful spots in Bedfordshire, regardless of weather or the seasons.

The next section is what is called a 'permitted way', and is not on the O.S. map, with the path at present by permission going through several 'kissing gates' and a most unusual chain scissor gate. If one wants, the G.R.W. can be regained by walking eastwards immediately on leaving Kings Wood. In any case the paths in this quarter are the subject of a diversion application, conveniently linking them; the other end of the link is met on the return loop. (A path out in the fields will then be 'extinguished').

We conclude this part through the pastures by going across a narrow field between wire fences, actually the buried route of a size 36 gas main. Just before moving on, look behind and see the range of hills,the subject of the earlier stage, quite striking. Right, through the kissing gate in the next 'paddock', and along the field's boundary on a very good grass path out onto the road.

Before going left down into the amorphous village of Houghton Conquest, take a look at the facade of the house up the slope which is called Rectory House; it is of Queen Anne form. The Ordnance Survey map shows a large moat on the southern side.

Go left again on reaching the through road called The Grove; no mistaking that the most important building in the village is the crenellated sandstone All Saints church. In these walks it might add extra interest if the walker makes comparisons with the churches on the Greensand Ridge; all use the same material, all have towers often with a spire and similar proportions for the naves. There is a stylish restaurant and wine bar opposite the church. For the next section the road is used which sets out into the fields, then on a sharp bend enter the arable fields at the How End F.P. sign for ½ mile. Actually the path is very narrow between two cultivated areas, though it is distinguishable, making in a straight line for a group of evergreen trees in a line of houses.

Now for the return, turning towards Houghton House on the hills. Don't be bothered by the sounds of gunfire at weekends, as the Chequers P.H. on Bedford road has a firing range for clay-pigeon shooting. Then on the termination of the present road, go through the gate onto the drive for Field Farm; there will be a yellow-tipped F.P. sign here. Walk towards the timbered farmhouse and at the rear is a rather woe-begone barn, showing missing planks though fully tiled – what about renovation?

Stay in this field, leaving the track, and away from the steading joined by a brook and hedge by your L.H.S.; a word of warning as the path very likely will be 'ploughed-out'. On reaching the top hedgerow go through and skirt the L.H. pond encircled by trees, and now C.W. round this field in the direciton of our objective. (This turning point is the junction with the proposed diverted path, seen earlier coming from Kings Wood).

In meeting the next hedgerow L. over the culvert, for these are all drainage ditches from the hill's watershed, and right after a few yards at a gate carrying on alongside another ditch, which has a cluster of trees around the head-waters; there is a bend of sorts, or a corner, where we change direction.

Houghton House goes almost out of sight, hidden by the brow of the rise, but we enter a horse-field over a gate and keep by the watercourse L. (Don't attempt going through the fence at the rear of Houghton House as there is no right of way).

In ascending these last stages Houghton Park House and its stables command the right flank and the field is left by means of a gate beside a pond. And so up the concrete drive, realising we are now close by the shell of Houghton House. This road bears round back to where the walk starts, and there is a further chance for the little extension down to the 'House' to take in the views, admire the fabric and sit out on the greensward.

Oxen, Virgates, Reeves and Burgages of Yesteryear

Places included: AMPTHILL – MILLBROOK – LIDLINGTON

Length of walk: 7¼ miles.

Grid Ref: Sheet 153 028 382.

Parking: In the western end of Ampthill Park car park or in lay-bys on the B580.

Bus services: 142, 143 and 145.

Public Houses: The Chequers (Millbrook), Green Man (Lidlington) and pubs in Ampthill.

Walk Links: Combines well with Walk 17, using the path on the northern outlet from the Park.

Notes 1: This is a 'figure-of-eight' walk on the Greensand Ridge and can be adapted or extended in several directions using the local circular arrow-signed markers on posts.

2: Two features are manifest on this walk, firstly the vehicle testing track near at hand and the other the wide views out over Marston Vale, now with prominent lakes in the brick-clay pits.

OXEN, VIRGATES, REEVES AND BURGAGES OF YESTERYEAR

Modern man has come a long way from his ancestral rural roots and it's a few of the lesser known early factors that I want to touch upon here.

Oxen were being used for ploughing and as beasts of burden from antiquity right up to the end of the nineteenth century. A furlong – furrow long – of which there are eight to a mile, indicated the length of an oxen plough strip before resting or turning, for oxen had minds of their own and followed a regulated day. Because of soil conditions this remained for a long time a variable measure, as were the other units based on oxen work. Bovate (bovine relates to cattle) describes an area capable of being ploughed by an ox in a year and that other term, the virgate, the area for a pair of oxen. Then we have hide or carucate being for the area eight oxen can manage in a year, seldom more than 120 acres. Being as the farmer was without artificial fertilisers and pesticides the oxen scarcely stopped work.

Since time immemorial ploughing and the Christian calendar, punctuated with Saints' days, governed village life, beginning with Plough Monday, the first Monday after Epiphany, 6th January, when wheat stubble got

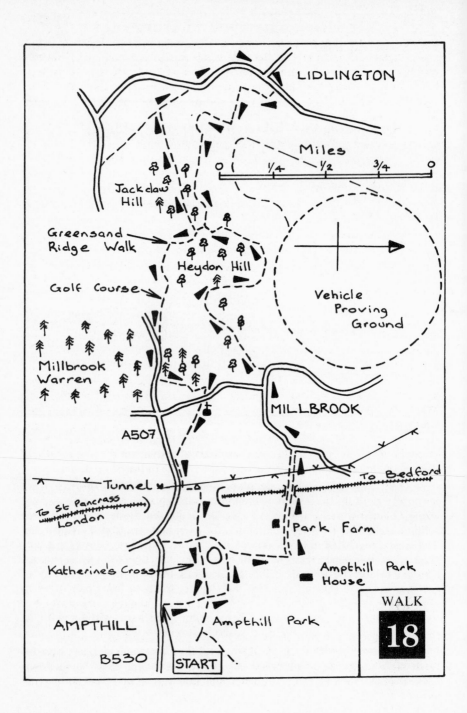

LIDLINGTON

Miles

0   ¼   ½   ¾   0

Jackdaw Hill

Greensand Ridge Walk

Golf Course

Heydon Hill

Vehicle Proving Ground

Millbrook Warren

MILLBROOK

A507

Tunnel

To Bedford

To St Pancras London

Park Farm

Katherine's Cross

Ampthill Park House

AMPTHILL

Ampthill Park

B530

START

WALK

18

turned ready for the spring sowing of barley, oats, peas or beans. Candlemass, 2nd February, marked the time when stock were excluded from the meadows as these were put down for hay. Lammas, 1st August, meant hay harvesting all being well and the return of stock grazing again for their valuable manure. Corn harvesting commenced about this time with Michaelmas, 29th September, expected as the end of harvesting when accounts could be settled. Come All Saints/All Hallows, 1st November, stock got driven from the fields under tillage and winter corn sown. Tethering of cattle on special strips of grassland was also employed in the big field systems, besides grazing on the commonland. Under the two and three field rotation system, fallow land had to be repeatedly manured and ploughed to destroy weeds, so the ox teams, often under collective ownership, never saw rest.

The term hundred signified an area in Plantagenet times supporting a hundred families, being comparable in size to the present day Districts. However, whatever your station in life, bordars, villeins, cottars or serfs all owed their existence to the Lord of the Manor, a title that did not get erased from the statute books until 1925. And the Lord held jurisdiction for dues, fines, laws and courts. Representatives of the hundred met in a central place, often in the open air, for the legislative moot court. A hundred reeve oversaw the court in the capacity of king's representative. In the larger administrative division of land, the shire, the shire's landowners' representative, became the Lord Lieutenant, and a High Sheriff was appointed by the crown representing the king's interests in the shire and ensuring the laws of the realm were enacted. (Sheriff being a corruption of Shire Reeve). Moot, loosely meaning meeting, did not die out with the collapse of the manorial system but got carried over in Tudor times when applied to the structure of boroughs. Tangible evidence of this is still to be seen in the form of a meeting room built over an open market supported on pillars, there being numerous examples spread throughout the country.

Whichever way one looked in the Middle Ages laws controlled one's life, either through the Court Leet or ecclesiastical court. These eventually evolved into the Court of Common Pleas in the thirteenth century, when common law held jurisdiction in civil disputes between subject and subject. The panoply of King's Bench courts, assizes and sessions took form, though for a while the Court of Star Chamber dealt with major disputes, especially if land was involved, before being abolished in 1641.

An extremely strong influence in country living throughout the centuries has been the churches and their parishes. Incumbents took tithes, invariably in the face of reluctance by parishioners who were always hard pressed, especially in lean years, and often with big families to support. In the course of time the parish took on poor relief work and highway maintenance after a fashion before the institution of toll roads. Glebe often appearing on maps or as place names indicates land directly owned by the church for the benefice.

From before Norman times 'borough' had its usage for large towns or villages, and with the subsequent enclosures for the next centuries that permitted abuse of privilege, most notable in the seventeenth century's 'rotten' boroughs. Let's not forget land begets power. Now the term burgage might not hold any significance in the present time, being the name once given to a long narrow plot of land with the roadside house built 'end on', found now in larger villages. The owner called a burgess had special voting rights and privileges, also specific duties in being a freeman or yeoman. When a 'town' under growth wanted to manage its own affairs it was the burgesses who were consulted, and they collectively made representation to the state pleading for a borough charter of incorporation. This enabled the creation of a mayor and corporation in the form of councillors and the more senior aldermen.

Prior to this form of local government one finds vestry committees, lords of the manor, reeves, courts leet and constables with an involvement in the running of a village/town. Constables were not solely law enforcement officers, for they had duties concerned with welfare, waste thrown into the street, sorting out offensive smells and collecting taxes. The business of trade and markets' control varied from place to place, highly complex and very explosive from every angle!

For administration in Bedfordshire and all its derivatives one has just got to read Joyce Godber's 'History of Bedfordshire', describing the unfolding of county life, and if one wanted to relate this county to the national scene over the centuries read 'English Social History' by G. M. Trevelyan.

WALK

18

AMPTHILL –MILLBROOK – LIDLINGTON

The walk commences at the Ampthill end of the football field near the changing rooms, heading off directly away from the road on the springy turf slope. Up onto the crest to meet the Greensand Ridge Way, whilst a few hundred yards away on the left stand two crosses. The first is in commemoration of Queen Catherine of Aragon, imprisoned during 1533 in Ampthill Castle which stood near this site. This spot was made famous in recent years as the place where the 'Masquerade Jewel', in the form of a hare created by Kit Williams, was discovered from cryptic clues in his book. The other cross remembers the dead in World War I.

A small wood stands overlooking a pond nestling in a natural amphitheatre, and we decend the slope ahead down to the boundary fence. Left here and follow it up to a stile, which is crossed by the path leading out towards the unmistakeable sight of the intrusive Stewartby brickworks chimneys. Near at hand stands Ampthill Park House, the product of several consecutive architects, principally John Lumley of Northampton (1704–07) and Sir William Chambers in the 1760s. Latterly it served as a

Cheshire Home and when the patients were transferred to the purpose-built building near the start of this walk, Park House was converted into flats.

The direction changes by bearing left on the well-surfaced track that passes on a farm's northern side. This intriguing farm building calls for a second look, having mixed brickwork styles typical of vernacular work, with dormer windows plus both tile and slate roofing, in a composition of differing elevations.

Staying on the bridleway brings us up to the railway bridge where the tunnel portals in the direction of London, St. Pancras, are seen, and in the other direction is Bedford. (Going over the tunnel is part of the walk's return). Passing over the bridge then immediately make a 45° crossing of the R.H. field to the road. (The track ahead is not a R. of W.). Turn left up the rising road into Millbrook where the houses in red brick Flemish bond have been given yellow window dressings and quoins, a sign that East Anglian brick manufacturing was not far away. The houses dated 1861 are part of the Bedford Estates.

'The Chequers' P.H. is situated close by the tee junction, though in fact we go on towards the entrance to the Millbrook Test Track. Built originally for General Motors, Bedford Trucks and Vauxhall Cars testing, complementing their Luton and Dunstable manufacturing and engineering plants, the track was bought by Lotus Cars in the mid-1980s. Just before the bend in the road go left beside a small stream; go through the car park and adopt the Greensand Ridge Way route. Above the tree-covered escarpment Millbrook's sandstone and coursed white stone church tower breaks the skyline, whilst we rise steadily on the firm path alongside sections of recent tree plantings.

On arrival at the golf course boundary fencing there is a sharp right turn, and a steep pitch is negotiated, with separately fenced lanes for walkers and riders. There is a curve round onto the picnic site on Heydon Hill, and the views make a break something of a reward for the ascent. In front are the vehicle proving circuits; beyond lies Stewartby Lake Country Park which can be visited from the A421 road, and further north the stretches of water in the vicinity of Kempston Hardwick are clearly visible. Eastwards on the escarpment the ruined shell of Houghton House, with Kings Wood behind, was the subject of the previous walk. On the slopes there are coverings of bracken and scattered trees.

Continue beside the golf course hedge, taking a right turn on meeting the G.R.W. sign around a short dog-leg skirting a small, almost hidden, pond, taking the clearly used trackway at the top of a steep, heavily wooded slope that is Jackdaw Hill, i.e. continue along the scarp edge and ignore other tracks leading off. (We come back through this trackway junction on the return).

This wooded section is lovely on a sunny day, with dappled lighting effects. It finishes at the edge of a modernised Bedford Estates house dated 1910. The gravel drive is the right of way, going forward and reaching a trackway crossing. We turn right here out in the fields, joining the road beside a complex of farm buildings.

Descend by the road which bends between high wooded banks, always on the watch out for vehicles, into Lidlington. Houses are strung out on the hillside; of particular interest are the 'eyebrow' thatched cottages, with the 'Green Man' P.H. near at hand. The newer estates parts of the village lie around the railway and towards the lake. This is the workings of the Brogborough brickworks, completely demolished in the late 1980s, situated close by Ridgemont station and the M1 motorway.

However, stay on the present road and look out for the bridleway sign beside a children's recreation ground. This next section of the walk has a pronounced uphill gradient for 200' alongside the test track fence, changing direction several times and passing by the village cemetery. Stay beside the test track, whilst on the R.H.S. the wooded slopes give an interest element – the outgoing path is along the top. There is, after something like ½ mile, a change of direction away from the track up a steep rise, joining up with the pond seen earlier. But this time we cross the stile in the hedgerow, entering the golf course.

Go forward carefully, crossing the fairways, staying on the R.H.S. of the pond which cannot be missed, using the yellow arrows on posts as a guide. After the pond change direction slightly leftwards, using the route of planted saplings which form an avenue separating the fairways and going down the whole length of the golf course in the direction of Ampthill. It will be noticed in doing so that the road gradually gets nearer and we leave by crossing the R.H. fairway at the end, and the now visible stile brings the walker out onto the road. Walk along on the roadside verges towards the Millbrook crossroads; now watch out for a footpath entering the pine woods just beyond the bend in the road. There are several paths leading away from the road, but take the middle one in the shallow vale, turning right at the bottom of the slope and leaving the woods on the path that goes right and out onto the road. The ground in this area is fenced and is inclined to be damp, as these are the catchment areas for the brook seen near the test track entrance by the G.R.W. sign.

Left up the road, then on reaching the bend take the G.R.W. on the other side, up a steep tarmac drive for St. Michael and All Saints church of Millbrook on its high spur about 400' above sea level. Before continuing on the track, take a look-about from this vantage point. Proceeding on, leave the vehicular drive on the bend, using the grassy path between two fences staying on the 'Way' now onwards. The roadside Dovart Kennels 'residents' will always start barking, so don't be surprised – the proprietors cater for boarding and breed German shepherd dogs. Our fenced path skirts a pond and changes direction again, now beside a wooded bank which is shortly crossed. This is the 'cut and cover' shallow railway tunnel, with the 'spoil' banked over the brick roofing.

Cross the stile and traverse the next field, which can be muddy, entering Ampthill Park by means of the bridge and stile. Rise up the slope ahead onto the skyline through the scattering of trees, and the two crosses come into view. Young trees are planted and protected in square enclosures in this enjoyable people's park, and when the outgoing path is met this is our cue for the last leg.

Bedfordshire's Buildings – Great and Small

Places included: WOBURN – MILTON BRYAN

Length of walk: 8 miles full circular or 5¼ miles for the shorter circular.

Grid Ref: Sheet 165 949 331.

Parking: Car park near Park entrance opposite the church.

Bus services: 160.

Public Houses: The Red Lion (Milton Bryan), Green Man (Eversholt, Church End), Royal Oak and other pubs in Woburn.

Walk Links 1: Battlesden Park and church through to Battlesden from Milton Bryan links Book 2 to Book 1 of these Bedfordshire Local Walks.

2: Using the Leighton Buzzard road out of Woburn A418, Walk 22 is encountered at Pinfold pond.

Notes 1: The full walk enables fine park land to be contrasted with agricultural cultivation, with a fascinating large Georgian village thrown in for good measure, not forgetting the magnificence of Woburn Abbey itself.

2: A perambulation of Woburn in all four directions is best done in the Spring before the crowds come, and there is an explanatory Heritage Centre with regular exhibitions. Need it be said, a tour of Woburn Abbey itself is a Bedfordshire 'must'.

3: Throughout this walk a 'B' surmounted by a coronet (Duke of Bedford) will be seen on many buildings.

4: Eversholt is famous in Bedfordshire for its 'end's' as a look at an O.S. map will confirm. Hills End, Tyrells End (house), Brook End, Church End, Wits End, Higher and Lower Rads End, Water End, Potters End, Higher and Lower Berry End and Wakes End (see notes in Book 1).

BEDFORDSHIRE'S BUILDINGS – GREAT AND SMALL

Buildings are one measure of man's activity in the countryside, so what might be relevant for those walking in and those visiting Bedfordshire? The following are only a few pointers which can be pursued by reading the growing book list for the county, which has many humble buildings and constructions and a few magnificent ones.

For a start, take a new look at railway and road bridges, especially those over the rivers; actually the 'Bedfordshire Magazine' has a lot to say on their histories. Then one can add canal-side buildings, police stations, cemetery chapels, lodge gates and associated dwellings, schools, etc., all examples of vernacular everyday buildings largely ignored by passersby. In the street furniture category we find post boxes, telephones, lamp standards, drinking troughs and fountains, war memorials, all giving character to our villages and towns. And so the list goes on, taking in municipal buildings, places of worship, then not forgetting the village shop, where it still survives, each with a unique tale to tell. Nor should we overlook archaeological sites with which Bedfordshire is well endowed; on this subject maps help enormously to pin down their exact locations, whilst more in-depth information can be gained from local societies.

Bedfordshire has no stone castles but there are several defensive earthworks of the 'motte and bailey' construction, notably at Yelden, Totternhoe and Bedford itself. Ecclesiastical establishments were founded at Beadlow, Bushmead, Chicksands, Cauldwell (Bedford), Dunstable – Priory and Friary, Elstow, Grovebury (Leighton Buzzard), Harrold, Millbrook, Newnham (Bedford), Old Warden and Woburn between the 10th and 15th centuries, though not all have much remaining above ground. As to churches, these are well recorded, particularly by Nikolaus Pevsner in his 'Bedfordshire and Huntingdon Architecture', and more recently good cameo descriptions by James Dyer in his 'Bedfordshire' guide. For excellent graphic penmanship there is Anthony Mackay's 'Journeys into Bedfordshire'. It would be wrong of me not to mention Eric Meadows' county photographic work of both churches and scenery, together with Bernard West's pen and word portraits of the villages. These appear regularly in the 'Bedfordshire Magazine' which has done so much over the years in keeping alive interest in the county's history and activities. But we digress.

For a secular building of special significance one would single out the Moot Hall on Elstow Green, a jettied timber-framed building comprised of a series of shops at ground level and a meeting room above. Elstow has many connections with John Bunyan, so fittingly nowadays it houses a museum for his life and times and also acts as a centre for Bedfordshire crafts. It has for company the village church across the green and restored timber-framed houses along the roadside. (See Village Greens in Book 1).

On a different note Stevington has a Scottish-like mercat cross whilst a

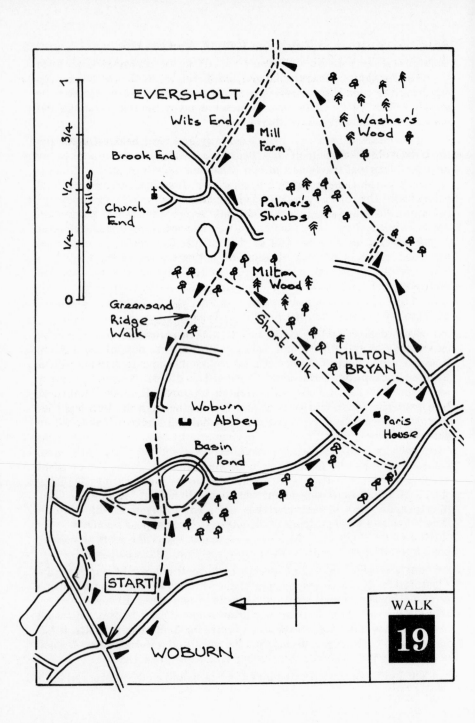

EVERSHOLT

Wits End

Brook End

Church End

Mill Farm

Washers' Wood

Palmer's Shrubs

Milton Wood

Greensand Ridge Walk

Short walk

MILTON BRYAN

Woburn Abbey

Basin Pond

Paris House

START

WOBURN

WALK

19

110

similar one stands in Knotting; then there are the Queen Katherine cross in Ampthill Park, and Leighton Buzzard's vaulted pentagonal market cross.

The handsome Houghton House, Ampthill, of 1615, and the equally ruinous Hillersdon Hall, Elstow Green built 1616, on an 'E' ground plan are on all visitors' lists. Of the same vintage a fragment remains of Bletsoe House, whilst Turvey Abbey also of this era survives intact.

The grandest building in the county must be Flitcroft and Holland's Woburn Abbey, whilst Luton Hoo House started from a classical design by Robert Adam, but mostly the work of Mewes attracts attention. Of a later date stands the 1834 stunning design of Wrest Park House, Silsoe, very much in the French manner, then one can add the notable lesser mansions lying along the Greensand Ridge. Of quite a different nature are the 16th century stables and the twin-bayed, crow-stepped gabled dove-house, providing nesting for 1,500 pigeons and open to the public in the summer months at Willington under the ownership of the National Trust.

On a more prosaic note, observed by all travellers through the mid-county are the brickworks south of Bedford. The Hoffman kilns, though low in stature, cover a considerable area, however one cannot fail to notice the groups of high chimneys and the obnoxious odours they disperse. Huge pits remain, though several now are open waters with public access like the Stewartby Lake Country Park, making the second series of lakes in the county. 'Brickmaking', a Bedfordshire County Council publication, makes informative reading and the topic is enlarged on in Book 1. Cement-making, also touched on in the companion walks book, was once a huge enterprise and now their kilns and chimneys have mostly gone, leaving great pits from the chalk extraction. The Totternhoe lime kilns do continue, though these have no chimneys.

WALK

19

WOBURN – MILTON BRYAN

Before setting out, take a look at the variety of buildings in the centre of Woburn, mostly 18th-19th century three-storey buildings with sash windows and in several instances cut-brickwork arch heads. In addition there are iron-work balconettes and contrasting brick dressings. The Market House is eye-catching and around this area the cobbles have been retained. Woburn has kept its 1951 Festival of Britain sign, a lasting Bedfordshire celebration in the small towns and villages.

We leave in the direction of Hockliffe down George Street from in front of the Bedford Arms Hotel, with yet more housing types occupying the eye. Just after a petrol station a broad avenue of trees sweeps across the road proving a 'frame' on the left for the Abbey, situated on the far side of a lake. Ivy Lodge stands almost unnoticed this end of the estate wall, where a G.R.W. post points the way through the iron gate and down a fenced path beside the avenue. Dogs must be kept on leads. Enter the park by the iron kissing gate, and since this is the junction with the last loop of the walk a short return into Woburn can be made.

Follow the route of the yellow arrows on short posts up the gentle rise to a ridge of trees ahead, whilst the G.R.W. veers off on your left. Basin lake, one of a system of artificial lakes in the park, sets off Flitcroft's and later Holland's 17th and 18th century facade. The path joins the road by the bridge, which is our next section; a ruined sandstone ice-house can be seen on the brow over on the left after a while. When the road turns left we leave it, taking the yellow arrow direction beside the fence of Paris House, said to be a Tudor-style pavilion for the British at a Paris Exhibition, but looking incongruous, more in keeping with the 'magpie' black and white buildings of Cheshire. An exit in the rear wall brings you out into a field, so go to the L.H. corner and it is decision time again, for if you wish the return route can be met by going ahead through the woods following the perimeter wall, (yellow arrow route at the stile and white gate).

Back at the stile, this time right up the slope outside the iron fenced woodland on headland making for a F.P. sign in a rough grass field at the top. (The true course of the path is direct from the gate in the wall and is always 'ploughed out'). The strange brick windowless plain-looking building was for R.A.F. wireless communications in WWII and the rough area was the site of billet huts. Do not go up to the building, for one thing there is no exit, being under water authority control, but change direction as indicated, down the concrete path which winds round until it heads for the church tower, joining the road between a pair of houses bearing a date of 1906 under a 'B' and a coronet.

By the Eversholt road now for a short distance, passing the church, for this is an anti-clockwise walk, leaving the few houses and out into the rolling, hedge-lined countryside. When the F.P. sign R. is met this can be used; there may not be a distinct path at the field's edge, but it leads out to a green lane in front of a wood belt and can be used. Alternatively, continue along the road a bit further, and just before the bend go down the bridleway, which can be muddy and rutted, and meet the same tree-line. Choose the path for preference.

Dog-leg left into the rear field, putting the hedge on your left; no green lane as it is ploughed-out, but a remnant is met on leaving the field beside the pheasant rearing copse. From this position make a straight line for Palmer's Shrubs, two fields to cross on the right of way, and it cannot be assured that the path is always trodden out. There is a plantation now connecting Palmer's Shrubs wood left and the corner of Washer's Wood, so the best way is to follow Palmer's Shrubs then halfway along the plantation is a stile which takes us across the belt. (The right of way is direct from the corner to the stile).

Enter this dark green coniferous corridor taking the R.H. path and at the end bear right and follow Washer's Wood in the next three fields. (Don't go inside, there is no path and since these woods are for commercial return there is often logging taking place). Actually, we only go part way in the third field, as we change direction and make for Woburn when the track from the northern side of the wood emerges. Go over the hilltop, joining a gravel drive for Mill Farm, one of those on the Bedford Estates, dated 1851; often one or other of the brassicas are cropped on these lands then out onto the road at Eversholt Church End. Before continuing the walk, may I recommend walking in front down to the church to admire the cluster of buildings in this quarter.

Take the road towards Milton Bryan, and on the first bend look for the G.R.W. sign into the park after a distance of ¼ mile or so from Church End. Now the park is traversed on the way marked G.R.W., which initially bears left heading for a double stile and bridge in the fields, not far away from the tree-lined Linden Lake. (Then the yellow arrow route is met, which is the end of the direct connection from Milton Wood). The brook feeding the lake is crossed by a concrete bridge, as is the field in front up to an evergreen tree-line. It can be clayey still on the G.R.W. which we stay on for the next stages, through the trees until a clear way out is easily found. Then comes our last risk of mud in making for the boundary deer-fence.

Posts mark the direction, rejoining the park road following the Abbey gardens and arboretum. The ditch on the edge of the gardens is called a ha-ha; this gives those inside an uninterrupted view into the countryside whilst preventing deer and cattle from jumping in. Glimpses of the Chinese dairy and grotto are gained in passing the rear entrance, as we go down alongside the car park. Continue on beyond the 'No Entry' road sign, then down the grassy slope of the deer park with our old friend the G.R.W. signs. Excellent close-up views of the Abbey front are a worthwhile experience, then cross the road on the same straight line, taking the northern side of Basin Lake. This now heads for the entry gate into the park by the avenue of trees, and we change direction again on another right of way; alternatively return the same way back into Woburn.

If you recall, this was the first choice of change of direction, so cross the avenue and proceed under the canopy of a row of trees by a fence, bringing us to the end of the Shoulder of Mutton Pond rejoining the road. This curves around the Bedford Estates Park Farm which is an impressive range of buildings, all performing specific functions in their times, as did the yards, (see Book 1 for notes on farms of this period). As a pleasing touch, the weather-vane is in the form of a cart-horse. Over on the right skyline can be seen the boundary of the safari park which can be visited from the Ridgmont entrance. Rallies of all sorts also take place in the park.

Instead of leaving the park by the road, follow the signs pointing to the camping centre, but on the last bend go onward into the woods at the F.P.

sign. This last woodland section fringes the end of the lake near the entrance gates, a better view of which is seen by the Lion Gates, the far end of which has a cable-car ride over the water. The last stretch into Woburn is beside the grandly built 1865 estate church of the 8th Duke of Bedford, conveniently placed by him within the village.

Bedfordshire Travel

Places included: LEIGHTON BUZZARD – THREE LOCKS – OLD LINSLADE

Length of walk: 6 miles.

Grid Ref: Sheet 165 892 283.

Parking: Ample space in the Three Locks Picnic Site car park. (Buckinghamshire C.C.), close by start at The Three Locks P.H.

Bus services: 160.

Public Houses: The Three Locks.

Walk Links: Footpaths of this walk into Stockgrove Park join Walk 21.

Notes 1: This walk can be started as an alternative in Leighton Buzzard, using the first section of the Greensand Ridge Walk and staying on the towpath by the canal. Or one could amalgamate Walks 19, 20, 21 and 22, using fragments of each with the Greensand Ridge Walk as the link, thereby devising your own long distance 'Greensand Ridge Circular'.

2: This Walk 20 contains a good variety of scenery awaiting discovery by you, the walker.

BEDFORDSHIRE TRAVEL

Anyone northward bound out of London likely as not will pass through or over Bedfordshire.

No doubt in the distant mists of time ancient trackways did exist on a north-south axis, but it is not until the coming of the Romans that we have a road in the regular sense. The Antonine Itinerary of 211–217 A.D. lists routes in the Roman Empire, three of them utilising the Watling Street, proof of its existance. This highway went to Chester via the outskirts of Leicester and Wroxeter. Nowadays it is known as the A5 and acts as a route for north Birmingham and beyond, serving diversionary purposes during difficulties on the M1 motorway. In the east strides the Great North Road (A1) making for Newcastle, thence proceeding onwards as a coastal road into Scotland's capital. Whilst up the middle of the county, taking a tortuous route, struggles the A6, passing through Luton, Bedford and Rushden then on into Nottingham.

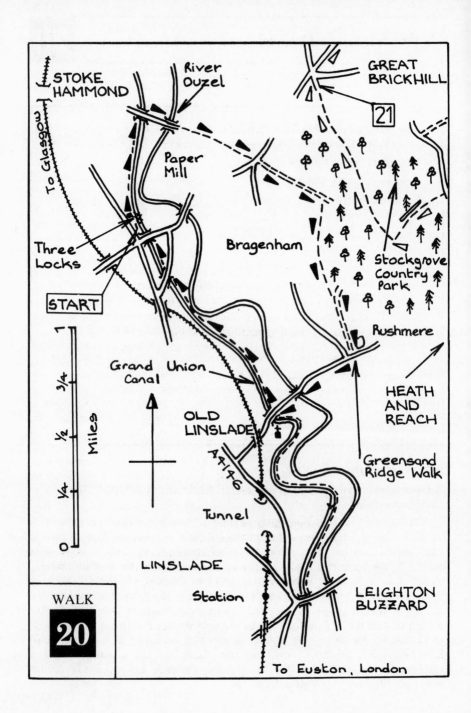

STOKE HAMMOND

River Ouzel

GREAT BRICKHILL

21

To Glasgow

Paper Mill

Three Locks

Bragenham

START

Stockgrove Country Park

Rushmere

1

Grand Union Canal

3/4

1/2

Miles

OLD LINSLADE

HEATH AND REACH

1/4

A4146

Greensand Ridge Walk

0

Tunnel

LINSLADE

Station

LEIGHTON BUZZARD

WALK

20

To Euston, London

Chronologically in terms of construction next comes the canal age of the mid-18th century onwards represented by the Grand Junction Canal, linking Brentford on the R. Thames with Braunston for Birmingham connections. Clay-lined canals measure on average 42 ft. on the surface and 28 ft. at the base with a typical depth of 5 ft. 6 in.; they hug the contours as much as possible 'locking' only when necessary, far excelling the horse and cart as bulk carriers, even though the horse was likewise the motive-power. When the canal companies of the midlands amalgamated the present name Grand Union came into being.

Moving on into the middle of the 19th century, railways proved from coal-hauling experiments in Northumberland a viable system, capable of generating business in their own right by ousting the canal barges for bulk carrying and the coaches on the roads for passenger carrying. Many houses with a slate roof were built after 1850, for it was railways that distributed Welsh slate the length and breadth of the land.

1831 saw the decision by the inhabitants of Leighton Buzzard agreeing to the coming of the railway. When built by 1838 it actually went through the parish of Linslade under the auspices of the London and North Western Railway Co., connecting London (Euston) with Manchester. Out in the eastern extremities of the county, Biggleswade and Sandy to be more precise, the Great Northern Railway Co. built their London (Kings Cross) route up to York, completed in 1852. A number of midland minor railway companies amalgamated their businesses to stimulate trade, but were forced to negotiate 'rail running' terms over the LNWR or GNR lines if they wanted journeys into London for their passengers and goods. Needless to say it was an unsatisfactory arrangement with their wagons sometimes waiting days in sidings, so a new route into London was a must. The Midland Railway Co. became the county's last major railway, taking a middle course through into the heart of England. Thus Nottingham, Leicester, Sheffield and Derby had their London Terminus, St. Pancras, in 1868, cleaving through Bedford and Luton.

Another 90 years on and the roads fight back in the form of motorways, Bedfordshire being among the first areas affected, for the M1 motorway initially started from Mill Hill in north London and finished at Hinkley in Leicestershire when opened in 1959. Subsequently extended considerably then integrated into the national motorway system, it has its problems even these days. Now, just out of the county in Hertfordshire, the M1 intersects with the M25, completed in 1988 and increasing the traffic volume on the M1 dramatically.

Railway and motorway civil engineering constructions have one thing in common, in that spoil taken from cuttings must be deposited as embankments and infilling. The M1 was built such that gradients and soil utilisations (slip-roads are part of the equation) were balanced in blocks of 12 mile sections.

Over Bedfordshire? Well, obviously the air routes. Luton's municipal airport within the London Airports' group handles large numbers of charter holiday flights, air-freighting, internal routes, private and business aircraft, not forgetting helicopter journeys. We ought to mention that they also have a flying club.

LEIGHTON BUZZARD – THREE LOCKS – OLD LINSLADE

This canal at Three Locks descends in a northward direction, and here stands a complex of a 1906 lock-keeper's cottage, a repair yard now in the iron-craft business and the well-known hostelry of that same name. In addition there is a good picnic site at the road junction nearby, managed by Bucks County Council.

Take the canal-side path on the pub side i.e. west side, even though the O.S. map shows the right of way as being on the other bank. At first the going is what might be called wet for there is no proper path; rounding the first bend a hoarding advertises Critchley's Fruit Farm on the other bank. From Leighton Buzzard through to Bletchley the River Ouzel meanders close by the far bank. Shortly the going improves as drainage ditches collect the surface water; hereabouts a milepost gives Braunston as 42 miles (32 miles as the crow flies). Our 'tow-path' crosses over onto the other bank at the Stoke Hammond road bridge, and here we leave the canal, going through the white Paper Mill Farm road gate, making sure it is shut behind us. The road goes over the Ouzel and the second bridge spans the mill tailrace. No wheel survives in situ, nor apparently any machinery, and the house is now a residence. No doubt paper was made at one time here for water powered more than just milling; even gunpowder manufacture needed harnessed water. It must be very wet at times in this area as the path is on raised boards near the buildings.

Up the gravel drive following the green arrows beside the covered stud farm yards, keeping in a direction away from the canal on an uphill bridleway. (There is a side bridleway left leading to Gt. Brickhill). Horse enclosures on both sides as we arrive on the hilltop from the stile by a gate. Here the path is in a depression, with scatterings of gorse and bracken, sure signs of the acid greensand soil, with a tree-planting scheme in evidence. From the top Milton Keynes takes the northern skyline, and in looking around we enjoy fine country views of tree-lined fields. Buckinghamshire and Hertfordshire do seem better at keeping their hedges than the farms of Bedfordshire.

Cross the road – there is a blue arrow marker on the bends – and enter the hollow way just before the Heath and Reach branch road. The brambles on the banks are the haunts of wrens. It is a bit rough on this sandy-stony path to begin with, sloping downwards to the woods ahead.

There must have been a fine row of majestic trees at the field's edge though only rotten stumps remain; maybe the owners could be persuaded that replacement trees would enhance the spot. No house can be seen which makes a change, and now a series of man-made ponds appear. Beware the anglers, for their lines can 'whip back' over the path when casting. A word of warning, the path is somewhat wet as it ascends to the woodlands, but in a couple of hundred yards the G.R.W. is encountered. We go right, following the good solid path, but in the forward direction the G.R.W. is making for Woburn close by Stockgrove Country Park, and this section is the link for Walk 21 in this book.

The going is good now for the rest of the walk, with plenty of varied scenery as you will discover, and not surprisingly an area that could be described as heathland, which is in fact the local name. (The Heath part of Heath and Reach). Young fir plantations are bounded by rabbit fencing, and a stile is crossed, then after a while the path descends through woodland, and it is near the bend that the G.R.W. diverts right off the path, so watch out for the arrow. The path comes close by a tree-lined drive and the expanse of Rushmere Lake comes into view – such a lovely spot on a sunny day. Listen for the coots.

The rear of the 20th century lodges and gates gets skirted, leaving by a side road gate and coming out onto a busy crossroads. If one wishes, the G.R.W. can be followed into Leighton Buzzard, well posted going up over the fir tree bank on the other side of the road.

Unfortunately, the next part is a road walk in front of Rushmere House – make sure you face the oncoming traffic by staying on the R.H.S. At the entrance to the Mill drive is a cast gear with wooden pegged teeth which could be replaced if broken or worn. Two bridges over the Ouzel then round the bend to the canal bridge, but, before progressing, take a look at the wharf on the Linslade side of the bridge; many can be found along canal banks serving local needs and in Leighton Buzzard's case taking away the quarried sand. The Old Linslade sandstone church stands impressive on a rise on a bend of the canal. However don't cross the canal bridge but go down onto the towpath on the northern side. We have the River Ouzel for company and in places the railway nearly looms overhead on the other bank. As a point of observation, look at the notches on the arch-irons of the roving bridge (a bridge that connects fields in the countryside) caused by the tow-ropes of the horse-drawn barges. Then, after a road bridge, the left bank is relieved by trees, constituting an excellent birdlife habitat, then on up to the Three Locks bridge, coming out beside the picnic site.

Countryside – The Sword of Damocles

Places included: HEATH AND REACH – GREAT BRICKHILL – LITTLE BRICKHILL.

Length of walk: 6¾ miles.

Grid Ref: Sheet 165 920 294.

Parking: Stockgrove Country Park. Access from A418 (Fox's Corner), Heath and Reach.

Bus services: 160.

Public Houses: Fox and Hounds (Watling Street A5), pubs in Heath and Reach and Great Brickhill, George and Dragon and Green Man (Little Brickhill).

Walk Links: Paths and bridleways in the Country Park meet Walk 20, and the paths in Lowe's Wood are used in Walk 22 but in the opposite direction.

Notes: Stockgrove Park has four distinct areas, namely Baker's Wood, an Oak woodland designated a S.S.S.I. growing with other deciduous trees; an open parkland found near the entrance; coniferous plantations encompassing the Park; and a stream feeding a lake system, making for a gentle encircling stroll, the usual activity in the Park. The Park is well endowed with flora and fauna, but please do not pick flowers as several species already do not grow there now because of this practice. All-in-all a fine spot for a leisurely afternoon on the Greensand Ridge; The County Ranger/Visitors' Centre is open with toilet facilities. A guidebook can be obtained.

COUNTRYSIDE – THE SWORD OF DAMOCLES

According to the Office of Population Census and Survey 41% of all adults say they went for a walk in the previous four weeks of their survey. This makes walking by far the most popular of all sports and recreations amounting to some 230 million walking excursions of all sorts a year, taken from figures compiled by the Ramblers' Association.

In times past just about everybody walked to work from the villages to the fields or to the mills and factories in towns. In these days of the car,

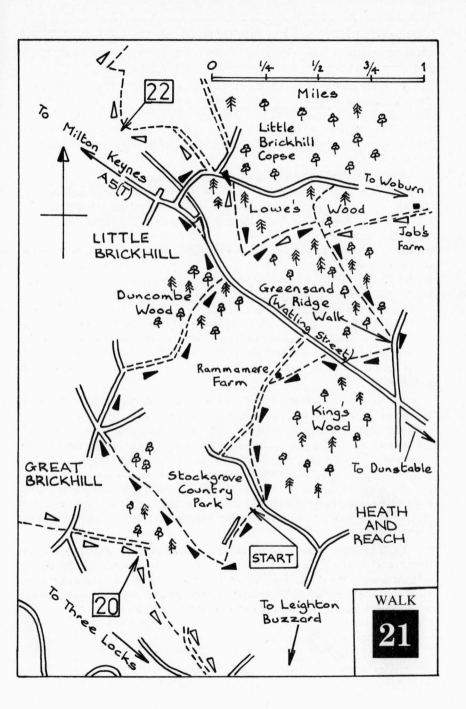

22

To Milton Keynes A5(T)

LITTLE BRICKHILL

Little Brickhill Copse

To Woburn

Lowe's Wood

Job's Farm

Duncombe Wood

Greensand Ridge Walk (Watling Street)

Rammamere Farm

King's Wood

To Dunstable

GREAT BRICKHILL

Stockgrove Country Park

HEATH AND REACH

START

20

To Three Locks

To Leighton Buzzard

WALK 21

walking features mainly as a recreation, especially when on holiday, and is an exercise strongly advocated by doctors, especially for those with heart problems.

Problems concerning the countryside might not be terribly well known. Take hedges for instance, so much part of our countryside, they have been disappearing at the rate of 12,500 miles per year. It will only take 20 years for hedges 'to be a feature of the past', and that's not scare-mongering, for the Jobs who prophesied the decline of village ponds have similarly proved to be right.

One cannot say that all is well with the 120,000 miles of footpaths and bridleways in this country for there are problems like ploughing-out, barbed-wire, overgrown hedges at stiles preventing usage. What about the major road schemes that scythe through path systems? Another fear comes about through the sale of the Forestry Commission woodlands and forests, for clauses should be written in allowing public usage of the rights of ways on these lands. Hitherto they have had good landowners and there's a legitimate worry that these two million acres could become 'no-go' areas overnight. One could find places such as the New Forest, Forest of Dean and Cannock Chase having public restrictions.

Members of the public are asked to report on footpath obstructions to the County Council, being invaluable for their problem-solving. It should be known that members of the Ramblers' Association, Conservation Corps, some Parish Councils, besides staff of the County Council, work to keep paths open.

It may not be generally known but the master maps for the country on paths are the Definitive Maps held by County Councils which keep up-to-date the rights of ways as a data bank to investigate problems. Now some authorities, not Bedfordshire, are seeking changes in the law by not making them obligatory. Should this notion find support, walkers face yet another hazard, for getting paths recorded onto maps has been no easy task and they are just about complete nationwide. Hopefully, the proposition will be found to be unacceptable, for it puts all footpaths at risk at a stroke and should be treated in the same manner as another idea of 'paying to walk' on certain paths.

On a brighter note County Councils are increasingly attaching greater importance to the matter of public access in the countryside and taking up related issues. What we don't ultimately want are simply a few hundred long distance paths in the country plus the circular county council walks, whilst the rest of the paths are withdrawn from public usage.

HEATH AND REACH – GREAT BRICKHILL – LITTLE BRICKHILL

Enter the pine woodland, at the rear of the toilets, onto a broad path with a good stony surface, finding that a gentle stream is by our side. The path is in a small vale and soon the stream enters an open stretch of water between tree-lined slopes. A splendid stone seat bearing the coat of arms of the Kroyer Kielberg family looks out across the lake to the foundations of a former boathouse on the other shore. (There is an excellent path on that side suitable for a circular excursion on the next visit). Rhododendrons grow near the lake along with a host of water margin plants.

Continue into the woods on the sandy path which cannot be mistaken, down the slope past the dam through mixed deciduous woodland, until a tee path junction is reached. Turn right up the steep slope beside the public boundary fence, crossing the vale's watercourse and leaving the Park by a stile on the crest displaying a yellow arrow. Take the broad path forward and do not deviate, passing on the way a small pasture field. The path in the woods undulates and a small sewerage station confirms we are on the correct way, and near here the Greensand Ridge Way is crossed. Forward, then shortly the path narrows considerably, becoming grassy to the end of the wood.

Leave by the stile and cross the next fields, staying by the 'sunken way' on your left, then down the slope, entering the tree-belt using the stile. Descend to the stream, and as the ground is soft hereabouts boards have been set-in providing a firm surface. This in turn leads us into a lane and so up into Great Brickhill village. If you have a penchant for timber-framed buildings there are several around these crossroads to attract your attention. (The Duncombe Arms P.H. is along the road in front).

Leave on the Little Brickhill road (R.) which means a good uphill tramp for about ½ mile, and on until the roads bend in Green End. There is no possibility of missing a pair of Victorian cottages, sentinel on a drive's entry with distinctive diamond leaded windows, lozenge scroll barge-boards and with visible tie-rod plates – nice to see the retention of these vernacular details.

The F.P. sign points the direction down this tarmac drive as we observe a cottage of 1777 vintage built in the 'M' or double-pile manner. Horses will be found in the vicinity, and the next part is on a gravel track crossing fields becoming hedge-lined in quite pleasant surroundings.

Care is needed or the path will not be found now, for at Duncombe Wood the track takes a rightward turn, but keep a sharp lookout for the white painted posts of the path's entrance into the woods. Although the grassy path is reasonably clear, nettles are encountered, and there are overgrown places as it is not managed, but walkers can help keep it passable. Watch out for the small pond, for who knows what insect and bird life might be about? The A5 main road is reached at the Lodge house gates and our yellow arrows reappear on the stile here.

Turn north on the A5 (Watling Street) in the direction of Little Brickhill on the roadside path for just over ¼ mile and into the long bend just before the village. Then on reaching the grass covered reservoirs take the road to Woburn on the new bypass flyover, then just after the first bend enter the plantation on your right. This is well used and clearly defined, taking you back toward the bypass, then on the perimeter trackway turn left and follow the route round a clockwise bend. After a short distance go left into a woodland drive approximately E.N.E. where the tree notice states 'private woodland'. The true right of way from the boundary drive in line with the entry path is absolutely impenetrable, so this alternative must be adopted. Muntjac deer sightings are possible in this area (seen by the writer), as are foxes and other mammals.

Keep on the drive, even though paths cross the way, and as a matter of interest the young tree plantations give variations in the tree canopy. Finally a broad way crosses the drive and is unmistakable for size, at which junction we turn right with a stand of chestnut trees now on your R.H.S. Shortly we meet up with the Greensand Ridge Way as it changes direction, and now this becomes the route back into Leighton Buzzard. We leave the area known as Lowe's Wood.

The indicating arrows guide our direction, with trees ranging from young spruce to elderly oaks. In the course of time the bridleway becomes a secluded grassy lane with wonderful sunlight effects as the rays filter through the leafy spread, and in the northerly direction fields reappear. Eventually this extensive section terminates on the Woburn road where we turn right. In a matter of yards the G.R.W. sign takes the walker back into the fields, making a diagonal traverse on a well trodden path in a westerly direction. A stile is crossed with a muntjac symbol and a small bridge, then strike out in the same alignment to the far hedge. Both these fields may have crops of rape or corn but do not worry as the path is official, and so out onto the A5, again marked by a F.P. sign.

Cross this very busy road carefully and look out for the G.R.W., just a little way north on the other side ascending the bank. Keep to the L.H.E. of the small fields and enter by the stile a very large sloping grazing field bounded by King's Wood, which is private. A change of direction as the fence on your R.H.S. is followed downhill, passing close by Rammamere Farm, and cross out onto the through track. We go left here whilst the other direction is another access route for the A5.

This firm stony track, that gives way to sand later on, enters woodland by means of gate and stile; bracken abounds and a generous sprinkling of coniferous trees confirm the acid soil.

When the pathway veers into a R.H. bend watch out for the Stockgrove Country Park sign for ½ mile and the yellow arrow for the L.H.S. It is a bit narrow in places with patches of gorse close by, and it looks as if we are making for a group of silver birch trees; two parallel paths form and the one on the right is advised.

Soon a stile shows up bearing the familiar yellow arrow and we enter open grassland in a shallow vale. This in turn brings the walker out onto the road opposite the Country Park entrance, so completing the circular and providing a taste of the Greensand Ridge Way countryside.

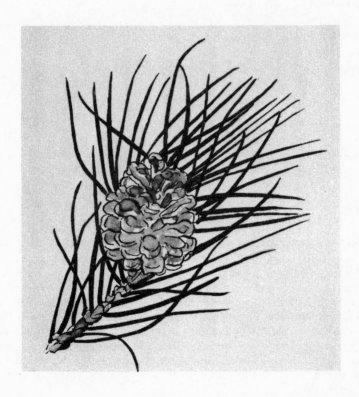

Paradise Lost

Places included: LITTLE BRICKHILL – BOW BRICKHILL –
WOBURN

Length of walk: 7 miles for the full circular and 3½ miles the
shorter version.

Grid Ref: Sheet 165 917 326.

Parking: Off road parking near the start point.

Bus Services: 160.

Public Houses: George and Dragon, also Green Man (Little
Brickhill), The Wheatsheaf (Bow Brickhill) and Birchmoor
Arms (Woburn).

Walk Links 1: The A418 Woburn to Leighton Buzzard picks up
with Walk 19 in the centre of Woburn, or the A5130 can also
be used.

2: Lowe's Wood on the southern side of this walk also appears
in Walk 21.

Notes 1: Mostly a walk in the pine woods on the Greensand Ridge,
marked by Milton Keynes occupying the north-western
skyline in the first leg.

2: The Wavenden Heaths are very popular for the short
distance casual stroller.

PARADISE LOST

**Christopher Wood's book on paintings of English country life and landscape
for the period 1850–1914, under the title 'Paradise Lost', offers truly
excellent reproductions of mostly less familiar paintings, for, as he remarks,
"the well-known paintings hanging in our galleries have had numerous
notes written on them and although they get the artists' biographies and
subjects correct they do not examine the very essence of the subject matter –
nor for that matter what has been deliberately left out". My paraphrasing
and condensation.**

**To Christopher Wood's credit he analyses the canvasses of the day by
pointing out the subtle hints reflecting reality which the artist allowed to
creep in to his or her work (Helen Allingham and a number of lesser known**

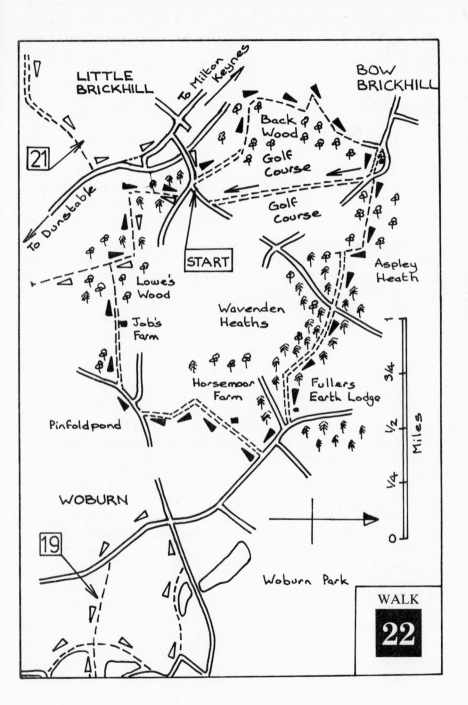

LITTLE BRICKHILL
To Milton Keynes
BOW BRICKHILL

Back Wood

21

Golf Course

To Dunstable

Golf Course

START

Aspley Heath

Lowe's Wood

Wavenden Heaths

Job's Farm

Horsemoor Farm

Fullers Earth Lodge

Pinfoldpond

1

3/4

WOBURN

1/2

Miles

19

1/4

Woburn Park

0

WALK

22

female painters were notable in their time) with or without the patron's permission. The subject matter in his text, from a social historian's standpoint, will probably be considered more important than the paintings themselves. What he sets out to expose is the difference between reality and what appears on the canvasses. Many of the water-colours were commissions or for consideration by 'hanging committees'. These 'committees' were largely academics who were looking out for the picturesque or visual composition rather than a commentary on the social injustices of rural life or the distressing lives the country people led.

Country people lived in damp, squalid hovels (and so did many of the folk living in the towns). Their long hours from dawn to dusk, and in the case of lacemakers working with expensive candles beyond that, were spent picking stones off fields, bird-scaring, hoeing weeds, potato picking and clamping, but these were not the subjects normally sought after by the artists' patrons. However, Sir George Clausen's subjects for his canvasses did depict toil, Sir Hubert von Herkomer shows the homeless on the road, John Brett and Henry Wallis both chose stone-breaking, a gruelling task, whilst Henry la Thangue and Frank Hall went so far as to depict death from hardship in the fields from ploughing.

So the supposed idyllic life in cottage gardens was not the norm, nor was that other popular subject with the galleries, that of milkmaids smiling at admiring swains. In truth the 'swain' would be a hired sheep-minder, sometimes spending weeks tending flocks, often moving the hurdles on his own and living in a cabin on iron wheels.

In this era Bedfordshire also had representative artists, one group being the Stannard family. The patronal head, Henry, saw the light of day in Eversholt in 1844, and his father also was an artist of some skill. Henry married Ruth Willshire in 1870 (born in Woburn in 1845) and their two sons and three daughters all became talented water-colour artists, Henry John Sylvester possibly being better known for signing his work as Harry Stannard. Furthermore, three of the grandchildren of the various marriages (all female) were artists in their own right.

The Bedfordshire Stannards seem not to have any connections with the brothers Joseph and Alfred Stannard, of the Norwich School of Painters. Their number also included the illustrious John Sell Cotman and John Crome, portrayers of rural life in somewhat poetic compositions, quite unlike the harsh reality of near-starvation of the long-suffering country people.

WALK

22

LITTLE BRICKHILL – BOW BRICKHILL – WOBURN

Commence the walk on the bridleway at the road junction. It can be rough as it is a timber-hauling track. The woodland is entered in the vicinity of a mixture of broom, gorse, rhododendron and great pines; signs of the big gales are evident with all the fallen trees. A stream is bridged as the path winds its way through the woodland. In a short while a pond is passed, with the sound of coots always pleasant through here. If, like me, you walk quietly, pheasants, rabbits, squirrels, foxes and an abundance of birdlife can all be seen, though in particular I keep my eyes open for muntjac deer. These either 'freeze' or, if upset, walk away.

After a section of plantations the way curves upwards through oak woods, though unfortunately the tranquility is spoilt by the noisy A5 road. Here in Back Wood follow the young plantation, turning in a direction towards Milton Keynes, but don't take the through path into the woods. One cannot help but observe the distinctive 'ridge and furrow' patterning in the fields below on the left, being almost certainly of mediaeval origin, for the herring-boned form we see is not that of steam ploughing that gave a similar effect.

Bow Brickhill can be omitted, but that would be a pity, so go and have a look at the pargetting, stonework, the timber-framing and the diaper-and-header bonded-brickwork. A few minutes' gaze from across the road at the Victorian village school affords such a collection of detail that several paragraphs of description would be needed. The Wheatsheaf P.H. is not far away at the Milton Keynes end of the village.

Return after your perambulations to Church Road and its varied complement of mostly English bonded houses, many of which are double fronted; yellow is contrasted with red bricks and if you look up you see the dentilations at the eaves, mostly dog-tooth work.

You will feel the uphill gradient making for the 160 m. level (530') on the map. Part way up the road takes an 'easing' gradient left, whilst the old line is followed as a minor road straight to the gate at the west tower of the church, and it then swings around on the southern side by the cemetery. Again, as expected, observe a sandstone building employing a number of dissimilar architectural details as in the square and ogee-curved window hoods.

If taking the option of the short route, go forward on the road just a short distance, when a broad sandy straight way is found angled off on your R.H.S., used by just about everyone visiting the woods, even if only for a little stroll. This takes you between Woburn's famous Duke and Duchess golf courses, arriving ultimately on a minor road requiring only a ½ mile walk R. back to the origin.

But the real purpose of this walk is in traversing the Wavenden Heaths and enjoying scenic variety. So go down the road below Bow Brickhill church and find the B.W. sign on the bend, then clamber up the banks ignoring the broad F.P. left. Soon there is a pallisade fence to go through, and then a stile sweeps round on the left side of the white house in the pines. Hoofprints should be a guide. Down into a steep gulley and up the wooden steps on the other side. Make sure you bear left on top of the last rise, for other paths lead off. With the ground falling away at your L.H.S. it curves clockwise, opening up to 8' wide under the trees. Go ahead on the B.W. crossing, coming out into a wide sandy fire-break on a junction of five ways on a brow.

There is no mistaking the main drive, being 12' or more broad and it later extends into more than 25' breadth, so go right here in a S.E. direction; the other side goes into Woburn Sands. This heathland walking reminds me of parts of the Surrey Hills around Dorking and Horsham on the sandy acid soils with their similar associated tree and plant life. At about the mile mark a fenced sandy drive crosses coming up from Aspley Guise, and in the next section we bowl along gradually losing height. (Don't take the yellow arrow path right when met). There is a change in the compass from east into north-east and we find outselves parallel with a road at the bottom of a wooded slope right. Trees abound throughout the heath in the plantations.

Dated 1884, the roadside lodge is an absolute fascination, with hung fish-scale tiles in a beautiful terrcotta colour, exquisite 'nail-head' patterning and a wealth of wire-cut brickwork. Even the chimneys have panelled stacks in low relief, there is a most impressive porch and the spandrels and barge-boards are decoratively fretted, all under a half-hipped roof. See this gem for yourself.

Turn towards Woburn on the road in a wooded cutting, using the far side path and ignoring the side road. When the road leaves the wooded section cross over and take the bridleway, setting out into the arable fields on a very good stony surface up into a farmyard. Though the farmhouse behind is but a dangerous shell of timber studding the 'bare bones', it shows graphically the structure of this type of building in this part of England; for instance Herefordshire timber-framed houses are altogether different. Go on through, entering a green lane that curves left into a vale but don't divert onto side paths. A nice mix of trees here by the stream. The A418 is duly met at Pinfold pond; the water was once at the site of the roadside pines and the front gardens of the two new large houses.

Turn right up the main road for a short way avoiding the Little Brickhill side road, meeting up with the G.R.W. just in front of a wooded brow. This good track yields yet another attractive area on the sand ridge, as it passes by Job's Farm with its white noggin brickwork in a timber framing and its thatched roof. Beyond it becomes a green lane, and if you are observant you will spot the field drainage outlets placed by the contractors in the ditches. Up the slope and back into the woods under the canopies of oak and beech – these 'kings and queens' of the English forest.

A crossing is reached where the G.R.W. turns left; instead you go right (north approx.) finding yourself on the link of Walk No. 21, but in the opposite direction. After a couple of hundred yards left into a broad fire-break; however, if you wish, you can go forward downhill to the road, then use it to go left back to the start.

Woods marked on maps cannot be trusted, as new ones appear, develop and are felled; the young oak and ash plantations are a case in point in this quarter. Stay on this break its whole length (there are several crossings), then on reaching the edge go right on the perimeter green way on the woodland's edge. It should be noted that the Bedford Estates have granted permitted-way status to the last section and the one we are now on. Curving round clockwise, arrive on a corner where there is a pond just inside the field; enter by the path into the coniferous blanketing so typical of this branch of forestry, being the final leg of the walk.

Bedfordshire Wildlife

Places included: CRANFIELD AREA

Length of walk: 5 miles.

Grid Ref: Sheet 153 955 420.

Parking: Near the church of St. Peter and Paul in Cranfield.

Bus services: 161, 163 and 164.

Public Houses: Carpenters Arms and Cross Keys (Cranfield).

Walk Link: Roads between Wood End and Lidlington for Walk 18.

Notes 1: The airfield at Cranfield has plenty of activity which includes biplanes, light aircraft, gliding and parachuting.

2: The Brogborough Hill Picnic Site, set out with combined seats and tables, affords long distance views along the Marston Valley, taking in the lakes and the Greensand Ridge as the southern 'curtain'.

BEDFORDSHIRE WILDLIFE

One might say Bedfordshire has three main areas from a natural history standpoint, commencing with the Chalk Downland in the south of the county mentioned in Book 1. The other two are the celebrated Greensand Ridge and the River Gt. Ouse Valley along with other open waters throughout the county.

Since most people have only a rudimentary knowledge of wildlife, recognising little more than daisies, dandelions, blackbirds and robins, the 'Bedfordshire Wildlife' book serves as an excellent introduction to the county. Nature trail leaflets from the Beds. and Hunts. Wildlife Trust sites help the visitor identify species from descriptions at the observation points on the trails.

Bedfordshire's section of the Lower Greensand Ridge is part of a ridge rising in Dorset and disappearing into the Wash at Hunstanton, broken in many places by other rock forms as a look at a drift geology map will show. Though much of the heather has gone from the ridge, it serves as a useful 'indicator' still, with some fairly extensive areas as on Cooper's Hill, Ampthill, and in the vicinity of Heath and Reach. A look at an Ordnance Survey map will show woodlands throughout the Ridge, and, where clay sits

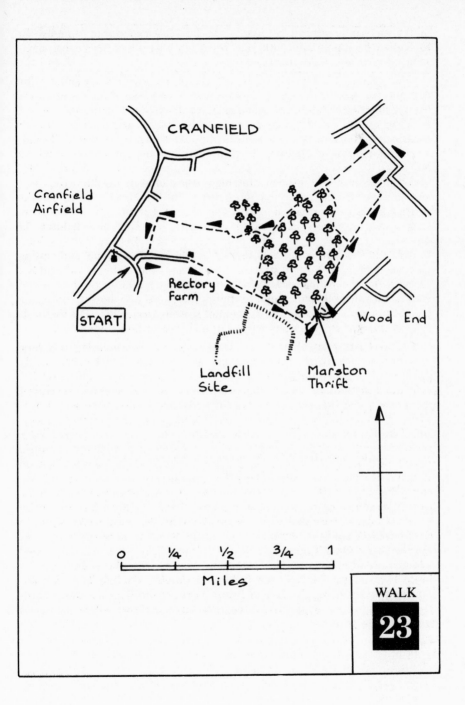

CRANFIELD

Cranfield
Airfield

START

Rectory
Farm

Landfill
Site

Marston
Thrift

Wood End

0   ¼   ½   ¾   1

Miles

WALK

23

133

on the surface, ponds can be found, as in the wet woodlands of Maulden. In this mixed deciduous and coniferous woodland a wealth of flora exists along with woodland-loving butterflies.

Soils along this 330–400 ft. high Ridge are not particularly suitable for agriculture, thus we see the great houses and the parks of the county here, leaving the better lands for farming. The outcropping sandstones are of building quality, so it comes as no surprise that it was used for church building and for domestic purposes in house building. But it is not all sand, as glacial deposits of Boulder Clay settled on the undulating crest, making for a varied scenery with an increased range of trees and plant life. Quarrying still does take place for high grade sand in Leighton Buzzard, and in the Flitwick area peat is extracted, whilst Fuller's earth for the woollen industry is extracted in the Clophill area. Fortunately some of these spent sites have been allowed to naturalise, creating new habitats of particular value for insect life, especially beetles. Disused railway lines become 'new' countryside, as witnessed at Old Warden Tunnel and cutting and the Sandy to Potton stretch. For variety and richness of wildlife, Flitwick Moor tops all county site lists, very much still on the Greensand Ridge. Categorised as a major wetland site there are mosses, flowering plants, fungi, moths, bugs, birds, amphibians and water life. The Bedford-shire Natural History Society carry out many recording studies here.

Gravel extraction along the Gt. Ouse valley for road building, war-time airfields and latterly new town construction created pits which subsequently filled with water. Although the river has its interest, it's these open stretches of water colonised by nature that were recognised as reserves, several of them now under the management of the Beds. and Hunts. Naturalist Trust, whilst the Harrold–Odell Country Park is managed by the County Country-side Rangers for the County Coucil. Besides fish, varieties of geese, water fowl, dragon-flies, toads and newts, all the familiar British birds and quite a number of foreign birds of passage, grass snakes, stoats, shrews, several varieties of willow and water-loving flowering plants grace the local waters. In hard winters northern wild fowl move south, when waters throughout the county serve as staging points for migratory birds. Bedfordshire has much to offer aspiring ornithologists, particularly at the open water sites. In addition there are several nature trails at the R.S.P.B. at Sandy Lodge. At the Harrold – Odell Country Park the Visitors' Centre has extremely good interpretive displays, plus fine panoramic views across the main water for bird observation. Similarly the Beds. and Cambs. Wildlife Trust's head-quarters, overlooking the lake in Priory Park, Bedford, has a comprehen-sive natural history display with regular lectures, and they will be pleased to welcome new members.

CRANFIELD AREA

Before setting out take a good look at both the church and the Victorian Gothic school, for I don't believe in haste at the outset. On the bend, pass the village hall and in a matter of few yards turn left into Rectory Farm road. From these high levels the Stewartby and Kempston Hardwick brickworks' chimneys are prominent and the distinctive outlines of the two airship hangars at Cardington can be seen to the N.E. In the foreground is one of the several old brickclay pits which are now stretches of water, becoming a transformed countryside, whilst the Greensand Ridge provides a pronounced backdrop to this area.

This walk takes in part of the recently designated Marston Vale Community Forest, with Holcot Wood lying due south but not included on this walk. The extensive landfill operation at the Shanks and McEwan site has necessitated the shortening of this walk from that described in the first edition.

Follow the road down hill to the red bricked double gabled Rectory Farm, continuing forward with the sound of running water in the nearby drainage channel. There's every likelihood of seeing teasels growing here. On reaching Marston Thrift we encounter the channel boundary of the old clay pit with the landfill within a boundary bank which should in the course of time be planted with trees. Our main interest is the wood itself and we go forward just inside the wood along the southern boundary to reach the road at Wood End and turn to the left. A map and signboard here gives a useful guide to this nature reservation.

Join the road, then on the first bend after only a matter of yards find the F.P. sign by the bungalow. This is a diverted path skirting round a donkey/pony paddock, though there is room enough by the trees; then for a short way enter the wood, returning into the next field. Marston Thrift is termed a S.S.S.I. (Site of Special Scientific Interest) managed by the Beds. and Cambs. Wildlife Trust, and in several places maps of the Thrift are post-mounted.

Beyond a pond the path enters the edge of the wood, continuing there until a fire-break cross-drive is met out of Wood End hamlet. According to the map the next bit should be in the field following the wood, but it depends upon whether the path inside the wood is cleared. Using the field get through the fence at the end of the wood. For now one can either take a short cut uphill at the northern end of the Thrift on a grass path or go forward. But as my intention is the encouragement of all path usage, the walker is asked to complete the next section even if the path is 'ploughed out'. Carry on in the same straight line away from the wood, but veer slightly left making for the L.H.E. of the nearest hedgerow in the field. Five poles for power cables stride across the field, so make for the middle one. Hopefully, as a result of this book, more paths will come into regular usage.

So now you know where you are, keep by this R.H. hedge, leaving this elongated 'L'-shaped field by means of a marked gap beside a yellow plastered timber-framed house of fine proportions. Forward on the road and A.C.W. up the hill and look for the bridleway sign between Hill Close and Hill Farm on top of the ridge. After doing a dog-leg behind the house the way enters the top of the last big field we walked through, and now there is a tremendous 180° panoramic view looking out over much of the country featured in this book of walks. Stay by the R.H. hedge, for this is the line of the bridleway which passes the rear of Hill Farm in the direction of the top corner of the Thrift. When there, the short cut is met, and there is a separation of riders from walkers by means of a wire fence, but be careful for the R.H. is barbed-wired. The muddy horse track shows how effective this is and it could be used in many more places. Although the Ordnance Survey map shows the bridleway as being inside the Thrift, actually it is outside.

On reaching the second wooded spur turn to the right, following its boundary up a slope which leaves the woodland to become a bridleway on the gentle rising ground towards the rear of houses in Cranfield.

A tee junction of bridleways is met here and we complete the circular walk by turning to the left and follow through to meet the outgoing Rectory Farm road.

Lost British Apples

Places included: TURVEY AREA

Length of walk: 6 miles.

Grid Ref: Sheet 153 941 524.

Parking: Near the Newton Lane junction with the through road in Turvey.

Bus services: X2 and X3 (both Northampton–Bedford).

Public Houses: Ye Three Fyshes, Kings Arms and The Swan (Turvey).

Walk Links: The Stevington Circular Walk 25 can be joined by roads to Duck End in Stevington or Rights of Way.

Notes 1: The River Great Ouse can only be seen at the outset, so make sure you sample the riverain scene from Turvey bridge. This is one of the six River Great Ouse walks in this book east of Bedford.

　2: A modern statue of the Virgin and Child is let into the end wall of Turvey Abbey beside the road.

　3: Stagsden Bird Gardens are not all that far away, featuring cranes, pheasants, peacocks and goodness knows what else. Why not go and see them with the family?

LOST BRITISH APPLES

Amazingly there were once reputed to be 6,000 varieties of apples growing in this country but now, like our ponds and hedgerows, orchards are diminishing at an alarming rate or are under threat. Only nine varieties dominate the shops and the threatened risks to Experimental Fruit Farms can only accelerate the decline of orchards (see Sword of Damocles).

Much of this decline comes from the fall of cider drinking since the 1950s. Wine drinking superceded cider, particularly from the 18th century onwards amongst the gentry. Farm workers, whether working in the harvest field or as part of their wages, drank cider by the gallon.

In 1883 there were reputed to be 1,500 varieties of apples grown in Britain, many to add a distinctive local flavour to cider making. Mediaeval and Tudor cooks knew all about cider for cooking and sousing, but in the reign of Elizabeth I people also acquired a taste for dessert apples, having enjoyed the types grown on the Continent.

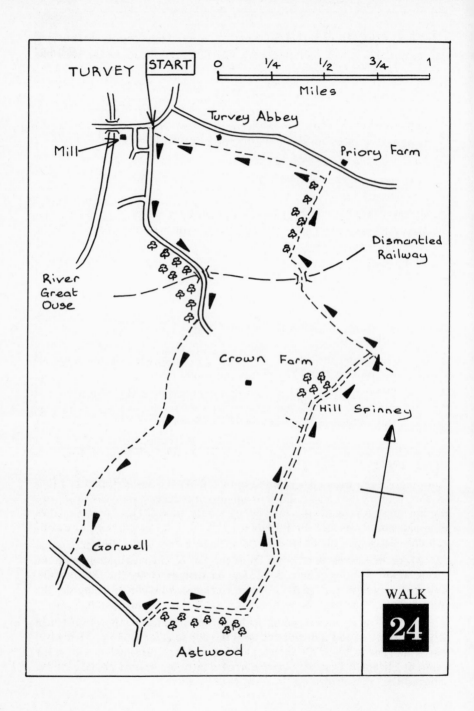

TURVEY

START

Turvey Abbey

Priory Farm

Mill

0   ¼   ½   ¾   1
Miles

Dismantled
Railway

River
Great
Ouse

Crown Farm

Hill Spinney

Gorwell

Astwood

WALK
24

138

Cider drinking – the real 'scrumpy' stuff – has now greatly diminished, accelerated by the fact that finding fruit-picking labour got increasingly harder. To offset this, keg-type cider and bottled brands made by the big manufacturers made something of a comeback. 'Common Ground' – mentioned already in connection with parish maps and boundaries – are campaigning to save some of these old orchards and plant new ones. There's an old belief that the cider tree needs 25 years agrowing, 25 years amaturing and 25 years adying, emphasising the need for continuous renewal.

Remarkably cider brandy distilling, with all these apples around and a world supremacy in the fruit, was last distilled in this country under licence in 1788. Elsewhere in the world the practice and consumption never faded, taking on all sorts of slang names. Now, after two centuries, Britain re-enters the cider brandy world when the products of The Somerset Cider Brandy Company come onto the market in 1991, joining Bulmer's 'King Offa' cider brandy.

WALK

24

TURVEY AREA

First see the river, for it's not seen during the walk, so go along the main road onto the bridge at a spot where the gently flowing river is not particularly wide. One notices too the splendidly renovated Turvey mill. From under the mill flows the mill race, overlooked by two incongruous statues named Jonah and his wife – long may they stay, (see 'Odd and Unusual Bedfordshire').

By the "Ye Three Fyshes" P.H. a remarkable stone building with an enclosed porch dated 1624 supported on pillars, one finds the lane by which we leave Turvey, and it's worth remarking upon the fact that the out-buildings of the pub are used by the diminutive Nix Wincott Brewery.

The walk proper starts out on the Newton Blossomville road. South on this road we come upon Lodge Cottage on the bend, distinguished by a Victorian balustrade porch and fretted barge-boards. Leave the road, taking a rising private road blessed with wide grass verges and dry-stone walling. The countryside takes the form of mixed arable and park land with hedges – top marks for their retention. On the turn, Long Belt, a great stretch of trees, literally divides the scenery, then round a wooded corner to cross the deep cutting of the dismantled railway, which we shall walk on later. Bide awhile here to look at nature. Most enjoyable scenery in all directions coming up to an excellent but lonely stone-built Keeper's Cottage, possessing a fine bracketed hood doorway, but sadly boarded up and unoccupied in its woodland setting. Unfortunately walkers are not permitted through Crown Farm when the road turns left, so we must continue southwards downhill on the grass slope, guided by the regular white B.W. markers.

A small correction in direction at a gateway, then cross a small field, with the B.W. route diverging on the left beside Gullet Wood. Views extend a good ten miles in this quarter and one gains a feeling of solitude because of the quiet, with not a building in sight. The grass bridleway comes out onto a road tee junction with Gorwelle House on the corner. Not far away two grid systems stride across the countryside, and we go on the side road in front of the house, a route punctuated at regular intervals by ash trees. Keep on this road, then when the bend south is reached take the bridleway again with the markers, going alongside the Astwood tree belt on the southern side – a haven for pheasant-rearing. Still on the broad grass ways take the northward direction as marked, when the field corner is reached which fringes Hill Spinney. The right of way bears slightly right onto a gravel surface track bordered by clipped hedges, meeting up with a tee junction where the big Turvey silos are not far away.

For the direct route back to Turvey turn left, then using the grass way for about half mile the way curves around a field corner to cross a redundant railway bridge at the tree-line. Bear left in the next field alongside the trees up to a wood plantation descending to your right, which is followed.

At the end of the tree belt the path enters an overgrown area, and watch-out for the stile on your left to gain entry into the field. Take a course parallel with the road through the fields towards the gates ahead, all the time watching out for sheep and cattle. In this area the route of the short version joins up at a gateway intersection and this takes us to a nearby bridge which is not crossed. With the stream course now on your right you will find linking paths in a continuous connection through small fields and ways, bringing you out into Newton Road where the walk commenced. On turning right, Nell's Well is seen, having a stone arch canopy bearing an inscription for the 1875 restoration saying that the reputation was 'the spring never runᶜ dry'.

Rural Skills – Basket-making and Thatching

Places included: STEVINGTON – The Stevington Windmill Circular.

Length of walk: 5¼ miles. 3½ miles short loop. Riverside extension into Pavenham resuming on the walk, 2½ miles extra. This would take you along possibly the loveliest river spot in Bedfordshire.

Grid Ref: Sheet 153 991 532.

Parking: Convenient dispersal parking in the village.

Bus services: 134 and 135.

Public Houses: Royal George and Red Lion (Stevington).

Walk Links: Bridleways through Pavenham and onto Walk 3. The road from Duck End out to the A428(T) meets Walk 24.

Notes 1: One of the finest walks in this book and thoroughly recommended, having plenty of variety.

2: Stevington Windmill, always in sight on this walk, is a fully restored post-mill that would have had common (cloth) sails, and is now in the charge of Bedfordshire C.C. Key arrangements for visitors can be made at the Royal George P.H. and particular instructions are displayed on the notice-board at the access road. A booklet is available recounting its history.

3: Stevington has a Holy Well seen on the return, an historic every-flowing spring beside the church. Good venacular buildings in stone, a handsome lion-headed hand pump with fluted column and surmounted by stylised fruit finial, then comes the famous village cross.

RURAL SKILLS – BASKET-MAKING AND THATCHING

Bedfordshire bobbin lace-making – still very much alive – and straw-plaiting were referred to in Book 1, so I would like to touch on those other county skills of basket-making and thatching.

Bedford, Biggleswade, Eaton Ford and Eaton Socon, Leighton Buzzard and Luton were all principal basket-making centres, serving particular needs, though most small towns had people in the trade. The firms often

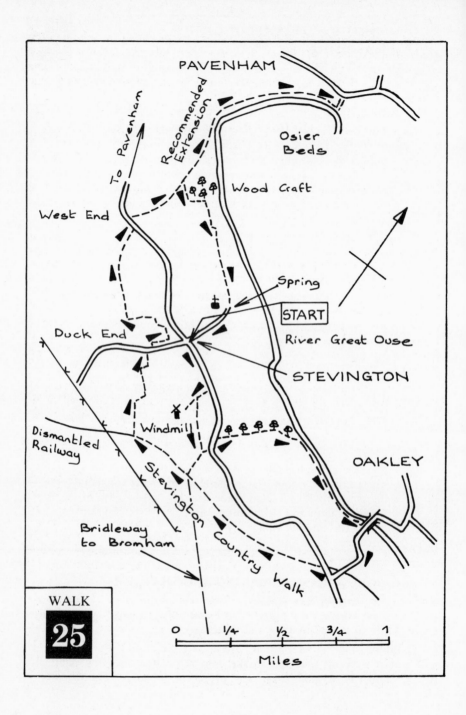

PAVENHAM

Recommended Extension

To Pavenham

Osier Beds

Wood Craft

West End

Spring

START

River Great Ouse

Duck End

STEVINGTON

Dismantled Railway

Windmill

Stevington Country Walk

OAKLEY

Bridleway to Bromham

WALK

25

0   ¼   ½   ¾   1

Miles

142

leased riverside lands for their osier beds or bought them through dealers, paying of the order of £12 for seven acres of river margins at Eaton Socon in 1913. The growing of osiers – a species of willow – and the making of baskets was added to the already established industry of rush-growing and mat-making already flourishing in Pavenham.

Cutting took place in the autumn, then made into bundles these were 'peeled' round about April time; it was considered a woman's job though very tough on the hands. After grading and re-bundling, they stood in wetlands to keep the sap going when peeled. Before weaving, the willow had to be soaked for several hours, then only the simplest of tools were needed. These hand tools were required for splitting, cutting and gripping, knocking the products into shape, then there were the bodkins of various sizes and grease-horns for lubricating the bodkins.

Fruit baskets or sieves in bushel or half bushel measures, skips, seedlips for hand broadcasting seed out in the fields, 'stikes', hat factory skips, watercress half flats for transportation, laundry baskets and 'Riddles'. Shapes included round, square or oval for shopping baskets, then there were cutlery boxes, food hampers, skeps for coal delivery and field gathering of potatoes, and pram and cycle baskets. Basket work found applications in the furniture world for wickerwork chairs, nursing chairs, baby cribs, bird cages, guards for carriage and cycle wheels, prams, pet baskets and eel traps. Fans, cots and basinettes (a form of pram) were basket made.

Baskets found their way into stables for a variety of uses in carrying and for feeds, and we must not overlook the round baskets used in the London vegetable markets, balanced on the heads of porters. Many of these were Bedfordshire produced with stencilled market gardeners' names on them for Covent Garden, Spitalfields, Stratford and the Smithfield meat market.

Thatching, the most traditional way of roofing, gave way to tiles in many areas, and with the coming of the railways in the mid-19th century Welsh slates spread across the country. A further difficulty arose with corn being cut by combined harvester, making the straw useless for thatching, consequently the number of practicing thatchers became fewer. Then came the revival when thatched cottages became desirable properties, so craft training schemes were initiated, overcoming the shortage of skilled men.

Nowadays, the older varieties of long straw wheat are grown again specially for thatching; rushes and reeds are considered better than wheat straw, with a life expectancy of two or three times longer, and it has to be imported to satisfy the demand. Heather and bracken can be used and rye straw is reckoned to be quite good. Thatching starts from the bottom right-hand corner. Very much a craft, with regional styles, the bundles of straw, called yealms, are held down by 'U' shaped hazel 'sways'. Ropes of twisted straw, split hazel and more recently binder-twine secure the yealms (and there are a lot of spellings and names for the bundles) across the roof. One method involves sewing the thatch down with giant needles, with an assistant working in the roof space, piercing the needle back to the outside. Using a 'leggat' (a bat with ridges or pegs), the thatcher will beat the thatch firm as he goes and finally the thatch is neatly trimmed all over with shears. The ridge having the distinctive regional designs actually overcomes the problem of making the apex watertight. This involves laying three rolls of straw or reed along the ridge, joining the layers of thatch coming up from each side. Another layer of straw is laid over the assemblage and strapped down each side by a variety of methods, then trimmed into one of the shapes, being basically functional rather than decorative. Straw has to be worked in a wet state, water being thrown onto the heaps on the ground, before the yealms are made up.

Quite a number of thatched houses can be found throughout the county, making for a harmonious amalgamation of building materials, especially when used with limestone as in the Gt. Ouse valley villages.

WALK

25

STEVINGTON – THE STEVINGTON WINDMILL CIRCULAR

Take the easterly direction out of Stevington on the Bromham road, keeping a look-out for Robert Shaftoe's organ building workshop, now in the Primitive Methodist 1863 chapel. Then, just before the first bend out of the village, turn right for the windmill (a road sign here), which opens most weekends in the summer months, otherwise key-holder information can be found on the notice-board at the roadside. For this walk cross the hard-standing of the farm forecourt, then onto the made-up track up to the mill, so you can go up and take photographs. Stevington's windmill will be seen throughout this walk. After this short excursion return to the edge of the farm, turning now onto the track parallel with the road, then on reaching the bridleway 'Tee' junction make back for the road. This particular track goes across the hill into Bromham and can be used as a 'Walks Link', crossed again later in this walk.

On the road again go towards Stevington for a short way, looking out for the F.P. sign by an iron gate near a bend on the other side. The big diagonal path shown on maps cannot be used, not being in existence, so we take the official diverted route which in any case is more scenic. From the gate down the well-kept track by the chestnut and oak treebelt, meeting the river by the Bedford Sailing club's enclosure for 'Mirror' class dinghies. Head for the Oakley bridge along the anglers' riverside path beside the reed beds, whilst on the far river bank glorious wooded landscaped grounds of private houses make a pleasant frieze. A cow meadow comes next, taking us up to the outside of fencing surrounding a weir spillway. Now cross the stile in the corner by the river, going out to the bridge under the trees. Before leaving this pleasant spot walk out onto the bridge and get a feel for the place, watching the weed rippling in the currents – the Water Authority's work is much in evidence. Several river access points can be found around the bridge on both banks.

Now comes a road walk away from the river, but be exceptionally careful on the bends and face the oncoming traffic. Recognisable are the tree banks of the dismantled railway, met on several of these walks, then on the road junction go in Stevington's direction, within a few yards as it were coming upon the Stevington Country Walk, having good roadside signposts used for our next stage. This Beds. C.C. site, utilising the old railway bed of the Bedford/Northampton line via Olney, has heaps of soil dumped in places deliberately with the intention of visually breaking-up the long straight stretches for colonising. Ash trees planted in clumps enhance the setting, making for a naturalising effect when they mature with the ballast taken away. Meadowland grasses and flowers colonise the old permanent way. Actually one enjoys the feel of a green way of broad green and high hedges and interspersed trees, so there's something for the botanist all the year round.

All through here one gets fine panoramic views out over the Ouse Valley on these raised railway banks, making for easy exhilerating walking. The Country Walk, divided into sections by wooden fencings, allows tracks for the fields; pass over the second one, being the Bromham pathway link mentioned earlier. The outline of a ruined railwayman's house can be discerned here. In the next section stop before the bend when the grid lines just come into sight ahead and look for the hidden stile R., just as the trees start again in the hedgerow. Further on the railway goes into cuttings near Turvey, utilised in Walk 24.

A downward grass path beside a hedge leads towards Duck End, the windmill now close at hand in the next field, then on reaching the bottom hedgerow R. crossing a plank bridge onto the well-trodden path, with great overhanging branches and the breadth signifying this was once a lane. Watch out for another plank bridge L. after 150 – 200 yards out of the trees into the field – be careful, it can easily be missed. Hereabouts trees are planted on waste ground on the far side of the R.H. hedge, then after several turnings we find outselves walking along the bottom mown lawns of bungalows. This becomes a narrow path out into Silver Street beside a garage which actually has a F.P. sign. Should you wish, the walk can be completed by returning into the centre of Stevington, but do go on if you have time. Across the street, just a little way right, a F.P. sign by a house called 'Fairview' gives a path leading out into the fields between houses; this entails following around the garden ends making an A.C.W. 'U' shape, picking up a stream on the way. We pass under a pole-mounted local power supply and reach a dung stack by the hedge, then cross the brook and go up the hill on the broad path to the top field corner. Go through the hedge in front here, bearing slightly right, coming onto the road by means of a stony way to the left of West End Farm.

On the road now left for a few steps, seeking the last white house No. 24 across the road; this has alongside it an overgrown F.P. sign signifying a grass lane which in turn becomes a footpath. Shortly the path enters a large field sloping towards the river; our way is beside the R.H. hedge, but don't go through the gap in the top corner. Going down this high hedge a decision must be taken as to whether the Pavenham extension will be undertaken.

Pavenham Extension. This has my vote as one of the most beautiful parts of Bedfordshire and is chosen for the cover of this book.

This path, now of broad proportions, fringes growing woodlands, having to cross a footbridge by the riverside, then taking the higher ground as one gets closer to Pavenham.

Grand circular. So, when the high hedge meets Wood Craft, find the gap in the hedge and the plank bridge, which can easily be missed, finding yourself in a short section of hedgerow.We emerge in a strip of green by the wood, but this is not the right of way. Enter the field at its top corner, crossing the wooden fence, which must be followed down to the river, continuing round the corner and then parallel with the river. Really a little disconcerting, but we escape on gaining the F.P. sign into a long meadow. This, with the 'Pavenham extension', provides one of those idyllic English pastoral settings, a slow, tree-lined river with a church tower standing proud above a canopy of leafy branches. The tranquil scene has sheep and cattle grazing, and the setting is completed by trees of differing hues each side of the river.

Through the gate into the next wider meadow with views down the river towards Oakley bridge, met earlier in the walk. An interesting ornamental tree belt is seen across the River Gt. Ouse. Make for the pedestrian gate below the church under a canopy of trees, still following the south western fence line. Leaving the river scenery, close by the church mound, a spring trickles forth, passing under the path into the pond surrounded by the overgrown rhubarb-like leaves of the butterbur plants. The church of St. Mary Virgin, built in limestone, has a somewhat plain tower, whilst the castellated nave has a partially ruined side aisle.

Continue up Church Road, containing lime-washed brick and stone cottages, all with a mixture of tile and thatch roofing, which as a collection must be considered one of the delights of Stevington; on the way we pass a good example of sympathetic barn conversion. For visual and vernacular reasons this last section, from the river onwards, is a very satisfactory conclusion for this multi-choice excursion.

Further Walking Areas

Bedfordshire County Council Walks.

Some twelve or more walks leaflets have been produced for the county, and copies can be obtained from all libraries and the Bedfordshire C.C. Country Parks.

Bedfordshire County Council Picnic Sites. Brogborough Hill; Daisy Bank east of Carlton; Deadman's Hill, Maulden Wood and Forty Lane on the Hinwick road can all be used as bases for your own excurions or just to take in the views. This and more countryside information can be found in the Bedfordshire C.C. leaflet 'Discover what's best in Bedfordshire'.

Bedfordshire Ley Lines. Pursuing this controversial subject will enlarge your knowledge of the middle reaches of the county. What they amount to are lines of alignment of ancient sites, which include castles, churches, barrows, stone circles and holy wells found to be connected in straight lines, this being more than mere coincidence for some people. Examples of them can be found throughout the country, and in recent times they have attracted a lot of interest, for there is a belief that they exerted a hidden power capable of guiding travellers in times past.

Bedfordshire has a crop of four such ley lines, intersecting in the middle of the county, warranting their inclusion in this book.

The longest alignment runs from the Moat House, Leagrave, to another moat at Tempsford, making nine sites through the nineteen miles; another commencing on Waulands Bank, near Luton, takes in eight sites through to Holwell Church in eight and a half miles. In the fifteen and a half miles from Westoning church, up to ten sites are cited, finishing with Ashwell church, Herts, and in seven miles five sites can be found through to Higham Gobion earthworks.

Interestingly these alignments intersect with each other in the proximity of Pulloxhill, Lower Gravenhurst and Drays Ditches. Worth pondering on, they are discussed at some length in the book 'Mysterious Britain'.

Clophill Area. A good linear walk can be made passing the old Clophill church ruin, then on the north side of Chicksands Wood and thence to Rowney Warren Wood and through to Shefford. The bridleway can easily be discerned on the O.S. map, and this becomes a link for Walk 16 and on into Walk 15.

Colmworth – Bolnhurst. An area of mostly minor roads and few paths in the country, but it makes good ground for devising your own circulars. Use the O.S. map Sheet 153.

147

Coopers Hill, Ampthill. A heathland S.S.S.I. good for short walks, but do exercise great care in respecting this fragile habitat.

Cranfield to Bromham. The bridleway here can be used as a linear walk or used for linking areas east of Bedford, clearly marked on the O.S. map.

East Bedfordshire Long Distance Circular. This part of the county in the vicinity of the conclusion of the Greensand Ridge Walk does not get well walked, so this circular has been devised by the author based on Walk 14. This involves using the bridleways from Biggleswade through to Wrestlingworth, then to East Hatley, then turning A.C.W. into Hatley St. George round by road and bridleway to Cockayne Hatley Wood. On next into Potton and return either via Sutton (20 miles) or Sandy Heath (22 miles) into Biggleswade.

Grafham Water. Paths and bridleways around the reservoir afford good opportunities for walking on the fringes of this multi-activity lake, some nine miles in all, taking in stretches of woodland, a little road walking, but most of the time by the waterside.

Greensand Ridge Walk. The route is described in an excellent leaflet produced by Bedfordshire C.C., starting in Leighton Buzzard and finishing in Gamlingay just over the county boundary into Cambridgeshire, and all way-marked with the muntjac deer symbol.

Greensand Ridge Long Distance Circular. The walks in this book from Leighton Buzzard to Three Locks and ultimately across into Woburn Park can be combined into a grand circular, varied at will and making for a 25 to 30 mile tour.

Kempston – Biddenham – Bromham. Access to the river can be gained either at Queen's Park, Bedford or Kempston Mill. The river bend makes for a good circular clockwise walk, taking in Biddenham church and village, then into Bromham visiting the Mill and Art Gallery, and what is more a map need not be used. This little outing's route can be extended through Bromham Park and over the hill, joining the Stevington Country Walk (Bedfordshire C.C. site) and Walk 25.

Leighton Buzzard Canal and Two Ridges Link. Very easy and rewarding tow path walking northwards on the beginning section of the Greensand Ridge Walk, but onward through Three Locks (Walk 20), Stoke Hammond and into Bletchley, even on to Cosgrove if so inclined.

In the other direction it's the Two Ridges Link, an apt name for a walk which connects the Greensand Ridge and the Ridgeway at Ivinghoe Beacon. Best follow the informative Buckinghamshire C.C. leaflet admirably describing this eight mile link. Incidentally, this is another connection for Book 1 and 2 of these Local Bedfordshire Walks. Alternatively one can continue on the tow path into Berkhamsted.

Maulden Woods. Forest trails commence from the lay-by on the A6(T) north of Deadman's Hill, Grid Ref. Sheet 153 074 394. This is a special mixed woodland nature reserve not far away from the Beds. C.C. picnic site.

North Buckinghamshire Way. Rising near Chequers in the Chilterns through Kimble, Quainton, by Aylesbury, the Claydens, finishing at Wolverton, is a recognised long distance walk, with a publication for assistance produced by the Ramblers' Association. The main feature being the Vale of Aylesbury with the Chiltern Hills as a 'backdrop'.

River Great Ouse, Wolverton. Start in the Country Park close by the station, following the surfaced laid-out paths by the riverside, going into Cosgrove where the Grafton Way is met, then a canal-side return can be made into Wolverton. On the way the River Tove joins the walker. A map will help, but is not absolutely necessary.

Silsoe. Such good bridlepaths exist in the vicinity of Wrest Park that the writer did not devise a walk here for the Park. Silsoe church makes a good start point and one can walk all the way through to Upper Gravenhurst.

Tiddenfoot Lake, Leighton Buzzard. On the Ivinghoe road out of Leighton Buzzard this spot, now a water-filled sand pit, has tree-planted banks and woodlands, being excellent for family strolls.

Upper Lea Valley Walk. The walk begins in Leagrave, following the river through Luton, and utilises the old Luton to Welwyn Garden City railway bed on to Leasey Bridge on the Wheathampstead road out of Lower Harpenden. Leaflets for these stretches available from Bedfordshire C.C. and the Upper Lea Valley Group, Harpenden.

Warden Warren, Old Warden. Another site on the Greensand Ridge that can be used as a connection between these walks or for general walking, but keep to the designated rights-of-ways. Rowney Wood, Old Warden and Sandy all have warrens on the Greensand Ridge, the name meaning places for keeping rabbits (coneys) in times of old, either in artificially created mounds or 'free' burrowing. Rabbits were an important source of fresh meat for the feudal lords, who employed a warrener to manage the lodges and feeding areas. This occupation along with the word 'warren' became surnames. Another warren is thought to have been used on Sharpenhoe Clappers near Luton.

Elsewhere in the book the reader has been recommended to seek out the River Gt. Ouse bridges, and likewise one should visit the north Bedfordshire churches. These fine buildings contain a microcosm of life, reflecting the issues of the locality and nationally, very much part of the 'real' Bedfordshire. Inside the church, furniture, memorials, regimental colours, stained glass and antiquities all have something to say, with the guarantee that no two churches are the same.

Selected Places of Interest

Aylesbury Museum.
Bedford Museum and Art Gallery.
Bromham Water Mill and Art Gallery. (picnic site by the river).
Bushmead Priory.
Canal Museum, Stoke Bruerne, Bucks.
Canons Ashby, Northants.
Castle Ashby, Northants.
Chicheley Hall, Newport Pagnell, Bucks.
Clophill, Old St. Mary's Church.
Elstow Moot Hall and Village Green, the church and Hillersdon Hall ruin.
Harrold, Lock-up and Market House.
Houghton House, Ampthill.
Leighton Buzzard Light Railway, Pages Park.
Luton Hoo House and Werner Collection.
Luton Museum and Art Gallery.
Luton Museum, Stockwood Park, (rural occupations' displays and the Mossman Collection of old carriages and coaches).
Olney, Bucks. (William Cowper, the poet, associations).
Priory Country Park, Bedford.
River Great Ouse Bridges.
Segenhoe Church.
Shuttleworth Vintage Aircraft Collection, Old Warden.
Silverstone Car Racing Circuit, Northants.
Stewartby Lake Country Park.
Stevington Windmill.
Sulgrave Manor, Northants, (George Washington's family seat).
Swiss Garden, Old Warden.
Willington Dovehouse and Stables, (National Trust).
Woburn Abbey.
Yelden Castle.

Further Reading

Arnold, James	The Shell Book of Country Crafts	David & Charles
Basham, Vaughan	Local Walks – South Beds. and North Chilterns	Book Castle
Beds. C.C. County Planning Dept.	Brickmaking – a history and gazeteer	Beds. C.C.
Beds. C.C. County Planning Dept.	Champion Trees of Bedfordshire	Beds. C.C.
Beds. C.C. County Planning Dept.	Glossary of Terms – historic landscape and archaeology	Beds. C.C.
Beds. Fed. of W.I.s	The Bedfordshire Village Book	Countryside Books
Bedfordshire Natural History Society	Bedfordshire Wildlife	Castlemead
Bell, Patricia	Belief in Bedfordshire	Belfry Press
Bord, Janet and Colin	Mysterious Britain	Paladin
Brunskill, R.W.	Vernacular Architecture	Faber
Bunker, Stephen	North Chilterns Camera, 1863–1954	Book Castle
Carroll, David	Leafing through Literature: Writers' Lives in Herts. and Beds.	Book Castle
Cirket, A.F.	Stevington Windmill	Beds. C.C.
Cox, Alan	Odd and Unusual Bedfordshire	Beds. C.C.
Dundrow, Michael	A Lasting Impression	Book Castle
Dyer, James	Bedfordshire	Shire
Elkington, John and Hailes, Julia	The Green Consumer Guide	Gollancz
Elkington, John and Hailes, Julia	The Green Consumer's Supermarket Guide	Gollancz
Evans, Vivienne	Folk – Characters and events in the history of Bedfordshire and Northamptonshire	Book Castle
Evans, Vivienne	History All Around	Book Castle
Godber, Joyce	History of Bedfordshire	Beds. C.C.
Godber, Joyce	The Story of Bedford	White Crescent Press
Greeves, Tom	Parish Maps	Common Ground Publications
Greeves, Tom	The Parish Boundary	Common Ground Publications
Grey, Peter	Villages of the Ouse	Barracuda Books
Hanson, Maurice	E for Additives	Thorsons
Hawes, Hugh	Bedfordshire Windmills	Beds. C.C.
Hill, Jack	The Complete Practical Book of Country Crafts	David and Charles

Holt, Ann	Making Tracks	Ramblers' Association
Horton, Edward	The Age of the Airship	Sidgwick and Jackson
Hoskins, W.G.	Making of the English Countryside	Penguin Books
Houfe, Simon	Old Bedfordshire	White Crescent Press
Houfe, Simon	Through Visitors Eyes: A Bedfordshire Anthology	Book Castle
Mackay, Anthony	Journeys into Bedfordshire	Book Castle
Meadows, Eric	Pictorial Guide to Bedfordshire	White Crescent Press
Meadows, Eric	Changes in our Landscape	Book Castle
Moon, Nick	Chiltern Walks: Hertfordshire, Bedfordshire and North Buckinghamshire	Book Castle
Moynihan, Liz	Bedfordshire Rambles	Countryside Books
Norwich, John Julius	The Architecture of Southern England	Macmillan
Pevsner, Nikolaus	Bedfordshire and Huntingdonshire	Penguin
Peters, J.E.C.	Discovering Traditional Farm Buildings	Shire
Pinnock, Roy	Between the Hills: The Story of Lilley, a Chiltern Village	Book Castle
Ramblers' Association	Footpaths – Rights of Passage in the Countryside, (leaflet)	Ramblers' Association
Ramblers' Association	Head for the Hills – The Right to Roam, (leaflet)	Ramblers' Association
Roberts, Mary	Farm of My Childhood, 1925-1947	Book Castle
Trevelyan, G.M.	English Social History	Penguin
Turner, W.J.	British Adventure, (ref. British Mountaineers chapter)	Collins
Ventry, Lord and Kolesnik, Eugene	Airship Saga	Blandford Press
Wildman, Richard	Bygone Bedford	White Crescent Press
Wilson, Ron	Country Air: Summer and Autumn	Book Castle
Wilson, Ron	Country Air: Winter and Spring	Book Castle
Wood, Christopher	Paradise Lost (19th and 20th cent. countryside paintings)	Barrie and Jenkins

Most towns and villages now have books of bygone times in pictures and local histories and enquiries at the bookshop or newsagent will yield the book titles. Town directories should not be overlooked for useful information, and the library will always be forthcoming with useful information.

Magazines

The 'Bedfordshire Magazine' published quarterly contains a miscellany of county life and history and is one of the best of its kind in the country, making for essential reading.

For more general reading the following have considerable merit: 'Country Walking', 'Country Living', 'Country Life', 'The Field' and 'Farmer's Weekly'.

Television regularly shows documentary programmes on countryside matters and the B.B.C. T.V. omnibus magazine 'Country File' takes in all possible topics.

Organisations

Walking

Bedford Ramblers' Club. (Bedford and District H.F. and C.H.A. Group)
Ivel Valley Group of the Ramblers' Association
Leighton Buzzard Group of the Ramblers' Association
North Bedfordshire Group of the Ramblers' Association
Ampthill Walkers
Youth Hostels Association
(ask at the local libraries for the names of Secretaries)

Countryside

Leisure Services Dept., Beds. C.C. – Open spaces and amenities responsibilities.

County Ranger Service, Beds. C.C. – Countryside caretakers, management schemes and public information, etc.

The National Trust, Thames and Chilterns Region, Hughenden Manor, High Wycombe, Bucks.

Beds. and Cambs. Wildlife Trust, Priory Country Park, Bedford – Own and manage countryside sites of special natural history interest, natural history education and countryside protection.

Rambling Holidays

Bedfordshire Farm & Country Holidays. Farms spread throughout the county catering specially for those visiting Bedfordshire, whether touring or needing a base for walking in the neighbouring area; all well situated. Excellent leaflet available, well illustrated.
Further information: Janet Must, Church Farm, Roxton, Bedford MK44 3EB.

Countrywide Holidays Association (C.H.A.), Birch Heys, Cromwell Range, Manchester M14 6HU.

Holiday Fellowship, (H.F.), Imperial House, Edgware Road, London NW9 5AL.

Ramblers' Holidays Ltd., P.O. Box 43, Welwyn Garden City, Herts.

Bus Services

The bus information given below is taken from the Bedfordshire County Council Bus Guides and is correct at the time of going to press. Routes however are periodically reviewed, changed, terminated or new ones created, therefore enquiry is advisable before your excursion.

Bus route nos. for walks

		Operator
X1	Northampton – Bedford – Gt. Barford – Roxton	UC
X2	Northampton – Bedford – Silsoe – Luton	Coachlink
X3	Bedford – Gt. Barford – St. Neots	UC
X4	Bedford – Bromham – Milton Keynes	UC
X50	Bedford – Clophill – Luton	Coachlink
X51	Bedford – Clophill – Luton	Coachlink
X52	Bedford – Clophill – Luton	Coachlink
63	Bedford – Ampthill – Dunstable	Buffalo
65	Bedford – Ampthill – Dunstable	Buffalo
69	Luton – Dunstable – Hockliffe – Leighton Buzzard	Buffalo
70	Luton – Dunstable Leighton Buzzard	Buffalo
75	Luton – Clophill – Flitwick	Buffalo
78	Luton – Barton – Shefford	Luton Bus
79	Luton – Barton – Shefford	Luton Bus
101	Bedford – Wootton	BRC
103	Bedford – Wootton	BRC
112	Bedford – Gt. Barford – St. Neots	Barfordian
113	Bedford – Wilstead	UC
115	Bedford – Kempston – Hall End	UC
124	Bedford – Sharnbrook – Rushden	UC
133	Bedford – Bromham	UC
134	Bedford – Bromham – Stevington – Harrold – Odell	UC
135	Bedford – Oakley – Pavenham – Harrold – Odell	UC
136	Bedford – Oakley – Pavenham – Harrold – Odell	UC
142	Bedford – Ampthill – Dunstable	UC
143	Bedford – Ampthill – Clophill	UC
144	Bedford – Clophill – Ampthill	UC
145	Bedford – Ampthill – Silsoe – Luton	UC
152	Bedford – Swineshead – St. Neots	Cedar
152	Bedford – Gt. Barford – St. Neots	UC
153	Bedford – Keysoe – Lt. Staughton	Cedar
154	Bedford – Colmworth – Staploe	Cedar

160	Bedford – Woburn Sands – Leighton Buzzard	Buffalo
161	Bedford – Marston Mortaine – Cranfield	BRC
163	Bedford – Marston Mortaine – Cranfield	BRC
164	Bedford – Marston Mortaine – Cranfield	BRC
164	Bedford – Cranfield College – Milton Keynes	UC
173	Biggleswade – Potton	UC
174	Biggleswade – Potton	UC
175	Biggleswade – Wrestlingworth – Arrington	UC
176	Bedford – Sandy – Biggleswade	UC
177	Bedford – Sandy – Biggleswade – Hitchin	UC
178	Bedford – Gt. Barford – Gamlingay	UC
179	Bedford – Sandy – Potton – Gamlingay	UC
180	Bedford – Sandy – Old Warden – Biggleswade	UC
181	Bedford – Shefford – Hitchin	UC
182	Bedford – Shefford – Hitchin	UC
845	Bedford – Shefford – Biggleswade	UC

Bus Operators

BRC	Buckinghamshire Road Car
UC	United Counties

Contents of the Companion Volume to this Book
LOCAL WALKS BOOK 1
SOUTH BEDFORDSHIRE AND NORTH CHILTERNS

Index Map for the Companion Volume to this Book
LOCAL WALKS BOOK 1
SOUTH BEDFORDSHIRE AND NORTH CHILTERNS

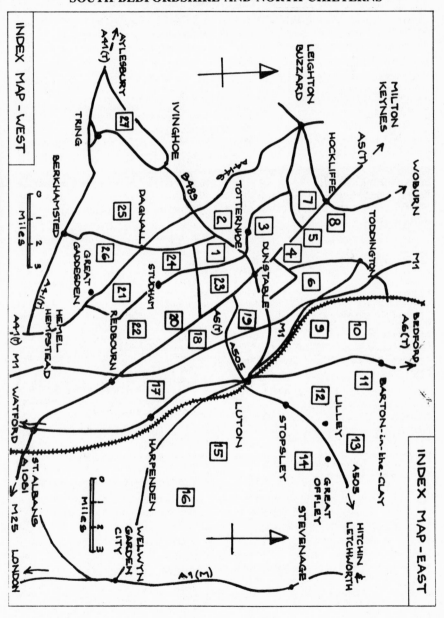

Index

KEY

Books Published by THE BOOK CASTLE

JOURNEYS INTO HERTFORDSHIRE: Anthony Mackay. Foreword by The Marquess of Salisbury, Hatfield House. Nearly 200 superbly detailed ink drawings depict the towns, buildings and landscape of this still predominantly rural county.

JOURNEYS INTO BEDFORDSHIRE: Anthony Mackay. Foreword by The Marquess of Tavistock, Woburn Abbey. A lavish book of over 150 evocative ink drawings.

NORTH CHILTERNS CAMERA, 1863–1954: From the Thurston Collection in Luton Museum: edited by Stephen Bunker. Rural landscapes, town views, studio pictures and unique royal portraits by the area's leading early photographer.

LEAFING THROUGH LITERATURE: Writers' Lives in Hertfordshire and Bedfordshire: David Carroll. Illustrated short biographies of many famous authors and their connections with these counties.

THROUGH VISITORS' EYES: A Bedfordshire Anthology: edited by Simon Houfe. Impressions of the county by famous visitors over the last four centuries, thematically arranged and illustrated with line drawings.

THE HILL OF THE MARTYR: An Architectural History of St. Albans Abbey: Eileen Roberts. Scholarly and readable chronological narrative history of Hertfordshire and Bedfordshire's famous cathedral. Fully illustrated with photographs and plans.

LOCAL WALKS: South Bedfordshire and North Chilterns: Vaughan Basham. Twenty-seven thematic circular walks.

LOCAL WALKS: North and Mid-Bedfordshire: Vaughan Basham. Twenty-five thematic circular walks.

CHILTERN WALKS: Hertfordshire, Bedfordshire and North Buckinghamshire: Nick Moon. Part of the trilogy of circular walks, in association with the Chiltern Society. Each volume contains thirty circular walks.

CHILTERN WALKS: Buckinghamshire: Nick Moon.

CHILTERN WALKS: Oxfordshire and West Buckinghamshire: Nick Moon.

OXFORDSHIRE WALKS: Oxford, the Cotswolds and the Cherwell Valley: Nick Moon. One of two volumes planned to complement Chiltern Walks: Oxfordshire and complete coverage of the county, in association with the Oxford Fieldpaths Society.

LEGACIES: Tales and Legends of Luton and the North Chilterns: Vic Lea. Twenty-five mysteries and stories based on fact, including Luton Town Football Club. Many photographs.

ECHOES: Tales And Legends of Bedfordshire and Hertfordshire Vic Lea. Thirty, compulsively retold historical incidents.

MURDERS and MYSTERIES, PEOPLE and PLOTS: A Buckinghamshire, Bedfordshire and Northamptonshire Miscellany: John Houghton. This fascinating book of true tales roams around three counties and covers three centuries.

BEDFORDSHIRE'S YESTERYEARS: The Family, Childhood and Schooldays: Brenda Fraser-Newstead. Unusual early 20th century reminiscences, with private photographs. Three further themed collections planned.

WHIPSNADE WILD ANIMAL PARK: 'MY AFRICA': Lucy Pendar. Foreword by Andrew Forbes. Introduction by Gerald Durrell. Inside story of sixty years of the Park's animals and people – full of anecdotes, photographs and drawings.

FARM OF MY CHILDHOOD, 1925–1947: Mary Roberts.
An almost vanished lifestyle on a remote farm near Flitwick.

A LASTING IMPRESSION: Michael Dundrow. An East End boy's wartime experiences as an evacuee on a Chilterns farm at Totternhoe.

EVA'S STORY: Chesham Since the Turn of the Century: Eva Rance
The ever-changing twentieth-century, especially the early years at her parents' general stores, Tebby's, in the High Street.

DUNSTABLE DECADE: THE EIGHTIES: – A Collection of Photographs:
Pat Lovering. A souvenir book of nearly 300 pictures of people and events in the 1980s.

DUNSTABLE IN DETAIL: Nigel Benson.
A hundred of the town's buildings and features, plus town trail map.

OLD DUNSTABLE: Bill Twaddle.
A new edition of this collection of early photographs.

BOURNE AND BRED: A Dunstable Boyhood Between the Wars:
Colin Bourne. An elegantly written, well-illustrated book capturing the spirit of the town over fifty years ago.

ROYAL HOUGHTON: Pat Lovering.
Illustrated history of Houghton Regis from the earliest times to the present.

COUNTRY AIR: SUMMER and AUTUMN: Ron Wilson.
The Radio Northampton presenter looks month by month at the countryside's wildlife, customs and lore.

COUNTRY AIR: WINTER and SPRING: Ron Wilson.
This companion volume completes the year in the countryside.

THE CHANGING FACE OF LUTON: An Illustrated History:
Stephen Bunker, Robin Holgate and Marian Nichols.
Luton's development from earliest times to the present busy industrial town. Illustrated in colour and monochrome. The three authors from Luton Museum are all experts in local history, archaeology, crafts and social history.

THE MEN WHO WORE STRAW HELMETS: Policing Luton, 1840–1974:
Tom Madigan. Meticulously chronicled history; dozens of rare photographs; author served Luton Police for nearly fifty years.

BETWEEN THE HILLS: The Story of Lilley, a Chiltern Village: Roy Pinnock.
A priceless piece of our heritage – the rural beauty remains but the customs and way of life described here have largely disappeared.

THE TALL HITCHIN SERGEANT: A Victorian Crime Novel based on fact:
Edgar Newman. Mixes real police officers and authentic background with an exciting storyline.

Further titles are in preparation.
All the above are available via any bookshop, or from the publisher and bookseller

THE BOOK CASTLE
12 Church Street, Dunstable, Bedfordshire, LU5 4RU
Tel: (0582) 605670